Motivational Leadership in Early Childhood Education

Motivational Leadership in Early Childhood Education

Lynn Marotz ■ Amy Lawson

WADSWORTH
CENGAGE Learning™

Australia • Brazil • Japan • Korea • Mexico • Singapore • Spain • United Kingdom • United States

Motivational Leadership in Early Childhood Education
Lynn R. Marotz and Amy Lawson

Vice President, Career Education SBU: Dawn Gerrain

Managing Editor:
Robert L. Serenka, Jr.

Senior Acquisitions Editor:
Erin O'Connor

Product Manager: Philip Mandl

Editorial Assistant:
Stephanie Kelly

Director of Production:
Wendy A. Troeger

Production Manager: J.P. Henkel

Content Project Manager:
Amber Leith

Technology Project Manager:
Sandy Charette

Director of Marketing:
Wendy E. Mapstone

Channel Manager: Kristin McNary

Cover Design: Suzanne Nelson

Composition: Interactive Composition Corporation

For product information and technology assistance, contact us at **Cengage Learning Customer & Sales Support, 1-800-354-9706**

For permission to use material from this text or product, submit all requests online at **www.cengage.com/permissions**
Further permissions questions can be e-mailed to **permissionrequest@cengage.com**

Library of Congress Catalog Number: 2006019931

ISBN-13: 978-1-4180-1868-9

ISBN-10: 1-4180-1868-6

Wadsworth Cengage Learning
20 Davis Drive
Belmont, CA 94002-3098
USA

Cengage Learning is a leading provider of customized learning solutions with office locations around the globe, including Singapore, the United Kingdom, Australia, Mexico, Brazil, and Japan. Locate your local office at **www.cengage.com/global**

Cengage Learning products are represented in Canada by Nelson Education, Ltd.

To learn more about Wadsworth, visit
www.cengage.com/wadsworth

Purchase any of our products at your local college store or at our preferred online store **www.cengagebrain.com**

Printed in the United States of America
3 4 5 6 13 12 11

Brief Table of Contents

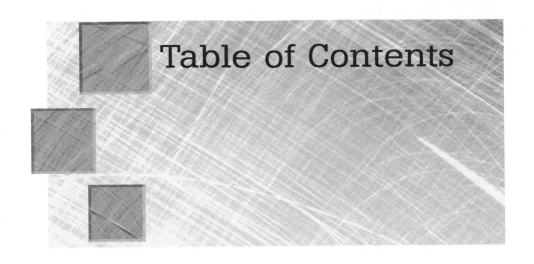

Table of Contents

Preface

Introduction

Leaders in any organization will tell you that one of their primary concerns is to keep employees motivated because it plays such a key role in employee recruitment and retention. However, motivational leadership is especially important to early childhood programs, in part because of the limited resources and challenging working conditions often present in such settings.

Despite the critical relationship to an organization's success, little has been written about motivation and motivational techniques that is relevant and appropriate to the field of early education. Numerous resources on the subject are readily available, but are typically written from a corporate perspective. Although the fundamental principles have universal application, the unique needs and conditions present in early childhood programs necessitate some sifting and winnowing to make the subject more applicable in these settings.

The Intended Audience

We have written *Motivational Leadership* specifically for early childhood leaders—those who are currently serving in leadership positions and those who are students in training. It is our goal to help you understand and appreciate the underlying theory, principles, and application of motivational strategies to improve employee morale, productivity, and long-term commitment. We believe *Motivational Leadership* has relevance for

- early childhood leaders who are working in a variety of settings.
- students pursuing early childhood degrees.
- individuals who are interested in developing leadership skills.
- trainers, in-service providers, and educational specialists.
- anyone who wants to learn effective motivational techniques.

 ## Organization and Content

We wrote *Motivational Leadership* with two assumptions in mind. First and foremost, we believe that *motivational leaders are found throughout every organization*. Although some may hold official titles, such as director or program coordinator, motivational leaders can also be office managers, head teachers, team leaders, or assistants. In other words, anyone who makes decisions, mentors, or encourages another employee's performance is displaying leadership qualities. It is this interpretation of the term *leader* that we will use as we discuss motivational leadership in this book.

The second point relates to the concept of motivation itself and its application in a workplace setting. Human behavior is motivated by a continuum of needs (e.g., physical, social, emotional, self-esteem) and the drive to satisfy these needs as they arise. Differences in personal experiences and backgrounds influence what individuals perceive as a need and what it takes to satisfy those needs. Thus, everyone's needs differ, and they typically change over time. Furthermore, motivation isn't simply an action, or a process, or something one person does to another. Rather, it is a *catalyst* that aids an individual in satisfying his or her own personal needs. Our purpose is to help the motivational leader develop and implement strategies that will, in turn, help employees gradually assume responsibility for self-motivation, which is the most lasting form of the motivational paradigm.

The material included in this edition is divided into two sections. Section I provides an overview of:

- current working conditions and factors contributing to an increasing demand for early education programs.
- why people work and what they want from their jobs.
- basic motivational theory and how this information can be used to meet employees' motivational needs.
- how leaders can use their skills and leadership styles to achieve outcomes.

In Section II, we focus on the application of motivational practices, including:

- practical and creative ideas for motivating employee success
- organizational incentives to encourage employee commitment and productivity
- strategies for addressing future leadership challenges

 ## Special Features

A number of special pedagogical features have been incorporated into this book to promote understanding, mastery, and application of the information provided, including:

- objectives and key terms to emphasize important concepts in each chapter; key terms are highlighted in the text and included in a comprehensive glossary at the end of the book.
- connecting points to help readers link chapter content to everyday situations.
- discussion points to stimulate critical thinking and encourage group discussions.
- an overview of prominent motivational theories to aid in an understanding of the purpose and importance of motivational leadership in the workplace.
- illustrations of motivational practices shared by exemplary leaders in the field.
- appendices containing additional resources and references.

Supplemental Materials

The CD-ROM that accompanies *Motivational Leadership* provides additional content and resource information designed to extend learning beyond the pages of this book. This value-added feature includes:

- worksheets to accompany the Application Activities in each chapter
- an extensive list of additional reading resources
- Web sites that provide guidelines for writing mission statements
- a printable list of motivational quotes
- Web addresses for a sampling of self-assessment tools
- guidelines for reflective listening

About the Authors

Lynn R. Marotz, Ph.D., R.N., is a faculty member in the Department of Applied Behavioral Science and also serves as the associate director of the Edna A. Hill Child Development Center at the University of Kansas. She brings her training and experience in administration, education, and nursing to the field of early childhood education. Her primary interests include teacher training, administration, and health promotion. She teaches undergraduate and graduate courses in administration and leadership, parenting, introduction to early childhood education, and health and nutrition. In addition, she has made numerous presentations at local, state, national, and international conferences, has authored numerous books and articles, and serves on a number of state initiative and policy development committees.

Amy Lawson, has a bachelor's degree in Human Development and Family Life/Early Childhood Education. She has 17 years of experience as a preschool teacher, child care administrator, and trainer. Her administrative experiences include university, corporate, and hospital on-site child care and early education programs for the children of employees and community families. In addition, she has served as the executive director of a nonprofit child care resource and referral agency. Currently, she is the director of the Seay Child Care Center at Presbyterian Hospital of Plano in Plano, Texas. For the past 10 years, she has presented numerous training sessions on leadership and motivation at local, state, and national conferences and always has large attendances—a testament to the tremendous interest in this topic and a tribute to her innovative approaches.

Acknowledgements

The authors would first like to recognize the early childhood leaders who currently practice a motivational leadership style and those who are interested in improving their motivational skills. Your dedicated efforts to attract, motivate, and retain outstanding teachers continue to enhance the quality of early childhood education.

The authors also wish to express their appreciation to a number of special people whose encouragement and technical assistance helped to bring this project to fruition. First and foremost, we are indebted to Cengage Learning and its outstanding Early Childhood Division editorial staff for their foresight in supporting a book on this important topic. We are especially grateful to Erin O'Connor, Philip Mandl, Stephanie Kelly, and the production staff for their encouragement, gentle prompting, guidance, and expertise in transforming an idea into reality. We also extend our sincere appreciation to the reviewers who contributed many invaluable comments and suggestions.

Jody Martin
Crème de la Crème
Golden, CO

Michelle Rupiper
Ruth Staples Lab School
University of Nebraska–Lincoln

Stacy Leighton
Creative Childcare Solutions
Seneca, SC

Kathleen Cranley Gallagher
Asst. Professor, School of Education
University of North Carolina at Chapel Hill

Karen Liebler
CEO, Children's Kastle Early Learning Centers
Lithia, FL

Marilyn Rice, M.Ed.
Director of Curriculum & Training, Tuckaway Child Development
and Early Education Centers
Richmond, VA

Maggie Connolly
Director, Frank Porter Graham Child Care Center at Frank Porter
Graham Child Development Institute
University of North Carolina at Chapel Hill

Motivational Leadership in Early Childhood Education

SECTION I
UNDERSTANDING MOTIVATION

Chapter 1

Early Childhood Settings: Unique Challenges in the Workplace

Objectives

After reading this chapter, you will be able to:

- explain how working conditions in early education programs contribute to employee turnover.
- describe several factors that often contribute to an employee's sense of job dissatisfaction.
- identify the classic signs of burnout.
- discuss several expectations employees have when they accept a job.
- discuss how leaders can use motivational strategies to attract and retain quality employees.

Key Terms

- attrition
- burnout
- collegiality
- demographic
- retention
- stress
- subjective
- T.E.A.C.H.
- turnover rate
- WAGE$®

> *"The vision is really about empowering workers, giving them all the information about what's going on so they can do a lot more than they've done in the past."*
>
> BILL GATES

 ## Introduction

The child care industry employs approximately 2.3 million caregivers and early education teachers (Center for the Child Care Workforce, 2004). Did you know that:

- of this number, approximately 75 percent are self-employed relatives or nonrelatives working in home-based settings?
- more than one-third of all positions involve part-time employment with no benefits?
- women between the ages of 20 and 44 make up 62 percent of the early childhood care and education workforce (Table 1-1) (Bureau of Labor Statistics, 2004)?
- early childhood teachers are among the lowest-paid employees in any given occupation?
- fewer than 31 percent have a college degree (Saluja, Early, & Clifford, 2002)?

Table 1-1   Percent of early childhood employees by age group (2002).

Age Group	Child Day Care Services	All Industries
Total	100.0	100.0
16 to 19	8.0	4.6
20 to 24	14.9	9.8
25 to 34	24.7	22.2
35 to 44	23.1	25.8
45 to 54	18.2	22.9
55 to 64	8.7	11.5
65 and older	2.4	3.2

Source: Bureau of Labor Statistics, U.S. Department of Labor, *Career Guide to Industries, 2004–05 Edition,* Child Daycare Services, (http://www.bls.gov/oco/cg/cgs032.htm).

As the field of early childhood education progresses toward achieving professional recognition and status, it continues to face many day-to-day workplace challenges. A major leadership concern in any organization is the recruitment and retention of talented employees, but it is an especially critical issue in the early education field. Motivational skills, the focus of this book, offer leaders an effective tool for attracting and retaining quality personnel.

In this chapter, we will examine important information about the employees who work in early childhood settings; leaders must understand their employees in order to be effective motivators. We will look at the fundamental reasons people choose to work and pursue careers in early childhood education. Finally, we will discuss what employees want and expect from their employers.

 ## Early Childhood Education as a Career Choice

What attracts people to the field of early childhood education? Why do some people find teaching young children a satisfying career choice? Most teachers identify children's laughter, enthusiasm for learning, and endless amazement as qualities that interest them in working with young children and their families (Liston, 2004; Papanastasiou & Papanastasiou, 1997). They describe their work as personally rewarding and fulfilling, and they find pleasure in introducing children to new ideas, encouraging their efforts, fostering their understanding, and nurturing their development (Figure 1-1).

Early childhood teachers, especially those with advanced training and experience, are increasingly finding their services in demand. New programs are opening while existing programs expand in response to social and **demographic** changes. According to the Bureau of Labor Statistics (2005), 70.4 percent of mothers with children under 18 years of age are currently employed in the labor force; 62.2 percent of these mothers have children younger than 6. These numbers are predicted to increase significantly in the coming years. In addition, some families are choosing to enroll their children in early education programs based on conclusive evidence that demonstrates the benefits of participating in quality early learning opportunities (National Research Council and Institute of Medicine, 2000; NICHD, 1998, 2000).

Figure 1-1 The joy of working with children draws teachers to the field.

Collectively, these changes are leading to a shortage of trained early childhood teachers (Bureau of Labor Statistics, 2005). This problem is compounded by the fact that a relatively high number of early childhood teachers leave the field each year, and fewer students are entering teacher-training programs, choosing instead to pursue other academic fields in higher-paying professions. The resulting teacher shortage will present early childhood program leaders with significant challenges and increase the urgency for understanding how to use motivation effectively to recruit and retain essential personnel.

Challenging Conditions

Retention of quality employees is a major concern for any business, but it has especially serious consequences for early childhood programs. According to the Center for the Child Care Workforce (2004), the annual **turnover rate** among early childhood teaching personnel is approximately 31 percent. This figure is nearly one and a half times higher than the average for U.S. businesses (Bureau of Labor Statistics, 2004). Employee loss results in substantial direct and indirect costs to an organization, including costs associated with recruiting, rehiring, and retraining new personnel.

In addition, it can cause a temporary disruption in the quality of service provided and contribute to low morale among the remaining employees.

Economic factors, however, are secondary to the negative and long-term effects that high staff turnover rates have on children's development (Helburn & Howes, 1996; National Research Council and Institute of Medicine, 2000; Rushton, 2001). Stable, consistent teacher–child relationships have been shown to be critical to children's emotional health and their ability to self-regulate behavior (Schore, 2001; Whitebrook, Phillips, & Howes, 1993). Frequent staff turnover produces a sense of loss and insecurity among children, and has also been linked to significant delays in their language and social development (Lamb, 2000; NICHD, 2000).

The Director's Showcase

What do you think healthy employee morale should look like in your program?

"I consider employee morale healthy when they are willing to stand behind an organization's mission—and are committed to meeting children's needs and those of the organization. It also means that employees feel comfortable discussing their problems, concerns, and ideas for change with me so they don't take these feelings home."

Michelle Scott
Early Education Program Director
Ballard Community Center, Lawrence, KS

So, why does early childhood education find itself in this predicament? What causes teachers to leave the field with such frequency? Unlike other forms of teaching, the care and education of young children present a number of unique challenges and responsibilities, including:

- meeting children's physical needs, such as feeding, toileting, and sleeping (Figure 1-2).
- serving a population with limited or no language, motor, or social skills.
- teaching and caring for children of multiple ages within a single group.

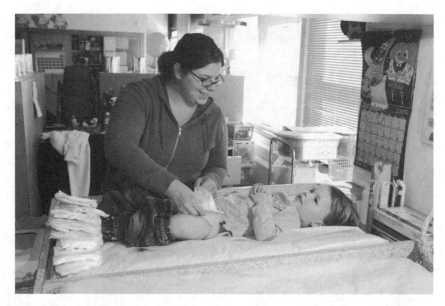

Figure 1-2 Early childhood teachers must meet young children's physical needs.

■ maintaining safe and healthful environments for young children who are at greater risk of injury and illness.

■ identifying children at risk for developmental problems, and arranging for appropriate intervention services.

In addition, the working conditions in many programs are often less than ideal. Some of the concerns frequently cited are:

■ long shifts that may involve 8–12 hours daily.

■ low wages.

■ lack of employee benefits, such as health insurance, retirement plans, paid vacation, and sick days.

■ lack of affordable training opportunities.

■ limited opportunities for advancement.

■ stress caused by emotionally and physically demanding responsibilities.

■ frequent personnel turnover and resulting staff shortages.

■ lack of professional recognition.

■ limited resources for purchasing supplies and equipment.

Some concerns, such as stress and long hours, arise from the very nature of the early childhood profession and will be addressed in later chapters. Others, like salaries, present a different challenge. Progress in addressing salary inequities has been difficult and slow due to a number of unrelated factors. One is gender-based: historically, women's salaries in almost all professions have lagged behind those of their male counterparts. Because women hold the majority of early childhood teacher positions, the salaries have traditionally remained low. A second factor is the lack of a uniform set of basic educational requirements for early childhood teachers, which makes it difficult to argue for, and justify, higher wages (Saluja, Early, & Clifford, 2002; Snow, Teleki, & Reguero-de-Atiles, 1996). Individual states are currently free to establish their own eligibility standards, which has led to much variability. In many states, a desire to work with children and the equivalent of a high school diploma are the only credentials necessary for employment in an early childhood program. However, as the overall level of teachers' educational preparation improves, appropriate compensation must follow. Third, a general misunderstanding about the critical role early childhood teachers play in fostering young children's development and an inaccurate assumption that "anyone can take care of children" impede public policy and support for salary improvements. Finally, high turnover rates continue to erode the strong bases of commitment necessary to achieve and maintain long-term changes. Although the early care and education industry is relatively large, it is not well organized, and consequently it has not presented a strong, unified front.

Connecting Points: Two months ago, you were hired as an assistant teacher in the toddler room at the See Saw Center. When the head teacher left for another position, the director asked you to take over her classroom responsibilities. This is your first job, and you've taken only a few early childhood classes at the local community college.

- How would you feel about being asked to assume the head teacher position?

- Would you feel adequately prepared to take on this level of responsibility? Why? Why not?

- If you decided not to accept the position, do you think your decision might jeopardize future opportunities for promotion? Explain.

- Assume that you are the director. What feelings would you have toward an employee who declined your request to take the head teacher position?

Workplace Challenges

Qualities that make the field of early childhood education attractive to teachers were mentioned at the beginning of this chapter. Among them are enthusiasm and the desire to make a difference in children's lives (Figure 1-3). For many teachers, the job remains energizing and fulfilling for years. However, others may become disillusioned and dissatisfied by the often-stressful working conditions and the demands involved in caring for young children. Some teachers feel their efforts and contributions are not appreciated. Others simply do not have adequate training or experience in early education and, thus, find themselves unprepared to develop meaningful learning environments or to manage children's difficult behavior in a positive way. Perceived and prolonged dissatisfaction with the job often motivates talented early childhood employees to leave and pursue other interests. In turn, the departure of friends

Figure 1-3 Teachers are often energized by children's enthusiasm.

and colleagues can contribute to a sense of loss, frustration, and low morale for the other employees. The resulting personnel shortages may also necessitate a reassignment of job responsibilities, which can increase the burden and stress on the remaining teachers.

Stress

Everyone experiences **stress** from time to time. We all talk about it in the workplace, often in a way that creates a negative atmosphere. A little reflection, though, reveals that stress is not always a bad quality. It may help spark interest, raise energy levels, improve productivity and performance, and keep us motivated in our personal and professional lives. An absence of stress is likely to leave us feeling bored and disinterested. Most people enjoy a certain amount of stress in their daily lives and, in many cases, actively seek it out, despite knowing that they may encounter obstacles along the way. For example, athletes train and compete, students return to enroll in challenging courses each semester, people move and begin new jobs, and novices attempt to learn a new skill or language or to play a musical instrument. Short-term stress can be invigorating. However, excessive or prolonged stress can lead to a range of psychological and physical problems (Jamison, Wallace, & Jamison, 2004). The key is to find a healthy balance between too little and too much stress in order to avoid its negative effects.

It is also important to understand that stress is an individualized experience and affects people in different ways (Figure 1-4). For example, two classroom teachers may encounter the same irate parent, yet react quite differently. One teacher may feel threatened and become visibly upset, while the other is able to empathize with the parent's complaints and calmly address her concerns. What causes each of these teachers to react differently to the same situation?

First, stress is a **subjective** response based on an individual's interpretation of an event and how it will affect her or him personally. Differences in personality, life experiences, abilities, and coping mechanisms cause people to perceive events as either threatening or manageable challenges. Thus, a director who announces that the program will open an hour earlier should not expect every teacher to be happy about the decision.

Second, the nature and number of additional stressors a person experiences can also influence reactions. For example, a lead teacher who has been without his assistant for several days due to

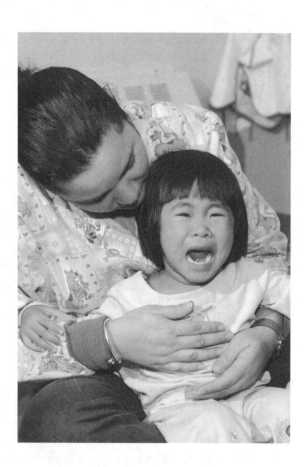

Figure 1-4 Working with young children can be stressful.

illness may become angry when the director informs him that she has enrolled two additional children with special needs in his classroom. Under ordinary circumstances, the teacher probably would not have responded in this fashion. However, the combined feelings of stress, frustration, and lack of control over the decision that has been made may cause him to react in an uncharacteristic fashion.

Studies have found that the more control individuals have in a given situation, the less stressful they perceive it to be (Bond & Bunce, 2001; Schaubroeck & Fink, 1999). Involving teachers in decisions that directly affect their work or personal lives can be an effective strategy for reducing the initial element of surprise and stress they may otherwise experience. Illness or pain, lack of sleep, personal problems, or an overextension of one's time and energies can also intensify a person's feelings of stress. Thus, to maintain good health and avoid early **burnout,** it is important for early childhood teachers and directors to learn and practice stress-reducing strategies in their daily lives (Figure 1-5).

▓ Take advantage of opportunities to learn new information and skills that will improve effectiveness on the job.

▓ Learn and practice time management strategies.

▓ Maintain a healthy lifestyle—get plenty of sleep, exercise daily, eat a nutritious diet.

▓ Develop new interests, hobbies, and other outlets for releasing tension.

▓ Join professional organizations, expand the network of contacts with other early childhood educators, and become an active advocate on behalf of young children.

▓ Be spontaneous on occasion—take an unplanned shopping trip, go for a walk, attend a sporting event, go out to eat, visit an art museum.

▓ Practice progressive relaxation techniques. Set aside a few minutes each day to relax and daydream.

▓ Set aside "me time" each day—read a favorite book, listen to music, watch a movie or favorite TV program, take a long walk, schedule a massage.

Figure 1-5 Stress-reduction strategies for teachers and directors.

Connecting Points: Think about your least favorite job as a salaried employee.

▓ What motivated you to look for the job?

▓ Why did you accept the position?

▓ Identify the factors that caused you to dislike the job.

▓ What motivators might your supervisor or administrator have offered to improve your job satisfaction?

Job Satisfaction

Chronic job stressors can take a toll on teachers' physical and emotional stamina and gradually lead to a condition known as burnout (Bright & Calabro, 1999; Murphy, 1996) (Figure 1-6). In the early stages of burnout, tardiness and absenteeism may occur frequently or teachers may be unwilling to assume, or volunteer for, any extra responsibilities. They may become defensive and make statements such as "I'm working as hard as I can" more frequently, even in casual conversations. Staff members may exhibit

An employee who is experiencing burnout may exhibit one or more of the following symptoms:

- loss of interest, creativity, and ability to concentrate
- increased feelings of not being appreciated
- increased complaining
- defensive behavior
- lack of energy
- difficulty sleeping
- loss of appetite
- inability to have fun
- decreased interaction and communication with other personnel
- depression or sadness
- frequent tardiness and absenteeism

Figure 1-6   Signs of potential burnout

a lack of motivation, increased irritability, resentment, and frequent complaining about working conditions, other staff, the director, or almost anything. Eventually, their commitment to the program begins to falter, and they may leave. Some employees experience burnout without feelings of frustration or stress. Their symptoms may extend to a loss of interest in routine work, repetitive tasks, or responsibilities that have little or no creativity associated with them.

There also appear to be critical times in a teacher's career when job dissatisfaction and early departure peak. The highest **attrition** rates occur during the first and fifth years, when teachers seem to make decisions about whether or not to remain with the same program or organization. However, the reasons for the first- and fifth-year decisions are quite different. First-year teachers are more likely to become frustrated with working conditions and job expectations and, thus, move on. Teachers who have remained with a program for four or five years may become disillusioned by a perceived lack of promotional opportunities or a feeling that their expectations have not been met. Consequently, they decide to either find another job in early education or abandon the field altogether and begin a new career.

Leaders in early childhood programs can anticipate and address many of these potential problems if they understand stress and its effect on employees' career decisions. Early recognition of behavioral clues often provides leaders with an opportunity to intervene before a situation reaches a possible crisis stage. Effective leaders will find that investing a small amount of time each day in such efforts can yield significant rewards in terms of rejuvenating teachers' careers and retaining quality employees (Curbow, Spratt, Ungaretti, McDonnell & Breckler, 2000). Numerous motivational strategies can be implemented to reduce employee stress, improve teachers' self-esteem, and create a fun work environment. Detailed descriptions of many different motivational approaches will be presented in subsequent chapters.

 ## Why Work?

People seek employment for a variety of reasons (Figure 1-7). Among the most common are:

- financial considerations and a reliable income
- personal fulfillment
- the opportunity to make professional contributions to an endeavor or program.

Each of these factors is subject to a host of other influences, such as an employee's career stage, cultural background, ethnicity, and the prestige and reinforcement associated with a position.

Many administrators and supervisors overlook important motivators that move people into the workforce. They fail to understand an individual employee's purpose for employment, and the reasons he or she has chosen to work for a particular program. Understanding that individual employees have different objectives for working is essential if leaders are to be effective in meeting motivational needs. For example, some employees depend on a reliable source of income to pay for basic living expenses or to make special purchases, such as a new car, travel, electronics, or hobbies. Employees who have families may feel a social obligation to hold down a secure job or to serve as a role model for their children. Consequently, employees who work for financial reasons are more likely to be motivated by a salary increase, bonus, or gift certificates for free movie rentals, restaurant meals, or health club memberships, whereas an employee who is fulfilling a social need may be more appreciative of a promotion or title change.

Figure 1-7 People work for a variety of reasons.

Some people enjoy working for reasons other than financial. They find work personally fulfilling and a way to validate their own feelings of self-worth. On-the-job performance provides an opportunity for such employees to display their skills and abilities. Their self-worth is validated through feedback and acknowledgement of their efforts by supervisors and colleagues. The workplace also provides an important forum for socializing and establishing friendships with colleagues who share similar interests. Leaders can create a work environment that these employees will find motivating by scheduling occasional social events, such as picnics, volleyball games, barbeques, sports outings, recognition dinners, birthday celebrations, or movie nights.

Still other employees have a strong desire to work in jobs where they can make a significant contribution. They prefer jobs that take advantage of their skills and provide relative workplace freedom and flexibility. Many such individuals find the teaching profession, especially the field of early education, an ideal career choice because they believe they can make a difference in children's lives. Given that teaching is a very people-oriented occupation, personal qualities such as nurturing, caring, patience, organizational skills, leadership, and creative abilities are highly desirable. Leaders can foster and support these characteristics by providing conditions that encourage autonomy, opportunities for skill advancement, appropriate challenges, assignments to special projects or responsibilities, and efforts to engage parents in children's education.

Understanding employees as individuals enhances a leader's ability to motivate performance and to create an environment that makes them want to stay. A leader's dedication enables her or him to deliver rewards that address an individual employee's real and perceived needs. For example, financial concerns may be a priority for the newly graduated teacher in his first job. In contrast, the teacher who has been with the same program for 15 years may prefer recognition and support for her work with children who have special needs.

The Director's Showcase

What motivational challenges are you currently facing?

"I am always trying to find ways to encourage staff to stay current in early childhood trends and developments, and to continue their education in early childhood. I continuously struggle with maintaining high standards of care and education and resisting the temptation to fall back into old routines because they are more comfortable. I try to encourage staff to think outside of the box, and to challenge children's development as well as their own."

Patricia Maddox, Director
Dealey Child Care Center
Presbyterian Hospital of Dallas, TX.

What Else Do Employees Want from Their Job?

Although employees' personal reasons for working differ, they often have similar expectations in terms of what they want from an employer, including:

- job security
- safe working conditions

■ recognition and acknowledgement of job performance
■ individual respect.

Job Security

Employees want assurance that their jobs will continue well into the future. This point may seem somewhat curious given the high teacher turnover rates and frequent program closures in the early education field. However, employees who are looking for job stability want the decision about whether to stay or leave a position to be their own. Leaders should acknowledge employees' concerns about job security and take measures to make their employees feel valued. For example, if a program does have the misfortune of closing, leaders should give employees ample warning and assist them in locating similar jobs in other programs.

Safe Working Conditions

State licensing standards help programs to establish environments that address employees' basic health and safety conditions. In addition, some programs choose to participate in one of several national accreditation initiatives offered by various professional organizations, such as the National Association for the Education of Young Children (NAEYC), National AfterSchool Association (NAA), National Association for Family Child Care (NAFCC), National Accreditation Commission for Early Care and Education Programs (NAC) administered by the National Association of Child Care Professionals (NACCP), and National Accreditation Council for Early Childhood Professional Personnel and Programs (NACECPPP). The goal of these and similar voluntary initiatives is to encourage and recognize quality early education programs that have met standards higher than those typically imposed by state licensing regulations.

Employees value their personal health and safety, and they expect employers to provide working environments that protect them from unnecessary harm (Figure 1-8). Although working with young children does have potential risks, such as exposure to communicable illnesses, injuries incurred from improper lifting of children, and occasional bumps, scratches, and bruises, employers can

Figure 1-8 Employees expect their working environment to be safe.

take steps to monitor the workplace environment and implement policies to protect workers' well-being (Bright & Calabro, 1999). For example, measures taken to reduce noise levels and maintain proper room temperatures contribute to teachers' comfort. Making sure adult-sized chairs are available for teachers and that countertops and changing tables are adult height can reduce the risk of muscle strain. Setting aside a quiet room, where teachers can relax and take a short break from classroom responsibilities, is also an effective strategy for reducing stress levels.

Recognition

Employees want meaningful work, and they want to feel that their efforts and contributions are appreciated. However, many leaders fail to recognize this essential need, find it difficult to put into practice, or do not devote sufficient time and effort to addressing it in the workplace. Understanding when and how to motivate employees plays a critical role in improving performance, reducing stress and job dissatisfaction, and preventing burnout. Acknowledgement of an individual's efforts through praise, a simple thank you, constructive feedback, job redesign, special assignments, or promotion goes a long way in expressing gratitude and making employees feel that their contributions are truly valued.

Connecting Points: Your teachers have been complaining about having trouble finding the outdoor play equipment because the storage room is in complete disarray. After hearing these complaints, you decided to come in on a Saturday morning and reorganize the room.

■ What were your motives for coming in on your own time to clean out the storage room? (Be honest.)

■ If no one noticed or thanked you for straightening up the storage room, how would you feel?

■ When others acknowledge your efforts, how does this affect your willingness to help them in the future?

■ Identify three or four situations in the past two months when you've acknowledged something special that another person has done, or you've complimented someone on her or his work.

Respect as an Individual

No two employees are exactly alike, and they need to be treated as individuals. Leaders should provide opportunities, such as assigning special projects or restructuring job responsibilities, for employees to develop and showcase their individual potentials. Then leaders must be sure to acknowledge employees' contributions. Programs ultimately benefit when leaders celebrate and support differences and create a climate of open communication and mutual respect. Such efforts also strengthen working relationships among employees and build **collegiality.**

Leaders must establish an atmosphere of dignity, understanding, and acceptance, and they should model the same exemplary behaviors (Figure 1-9). This is an especially important issue for leaders to address as the workforce and families served in early childhood programs become increasingly diverse. Harassment, stereotyping, discrimination, and insensitive comments and practices are unacceptable in the workplace and violate the NAEYC Code of Ethical Conduct (NAEYC, 2005). Such behaviors also lead children to believe that intolerance is acceptable.

Figure 1-9   Leaders should model exemplary behaviors.

 # Where Do We Go from Here?

Although early education programs continue to struggle with staff turnover and other workplace conditions, some improvements are slowly being implemented (Center for the Child Care Workforce, 2004). Newer initiatives, such as the **T.E.A.C.H.** Early Childhood® Project and **WAGE$®** Project, are designed to address problems of low wages, lack of teacher education and training, poor program quality, and high employee turnover rates. The effects of these initiatives on employee recruitment and retention are being monitored closely in hopes of building continued support and increased funding. Additional investments and program improvements are likely as policy makers and the public better understand the value of quality early education. In the interim, innovative leaders must focus their attention on practices that add to the attractiveness of early childhood education as a career. Such efforts will enable program administrators to attract and retain their best employees.

Summary

▪ Demand for quality early care and education programs continues to increase.

▪ Employee turnover rates are exceptionally high in the field of early education in comparison with other professions.

▪ Teachers are attracted to early education by a variety of factors, including the population of children and families served and opportunities to contribute to children's development.

▪ Retention of quality employees is an ongoing challenge that requires innovative leadership.

▪ Stressful working conditions, inadequate job preparation, and lack of recognition can lead to job dissatisfaction and early departure.

▪ People work for different reasons, including financial need, personal fulfillment, and a desire to contribute to the lives of children and families.

▪ Employees expect job security, safe working conditions, and recognition for their efforts.

▪ Adopting a motivational leadership style can yield positive outcomes, including improved employee morale and performance, increased commitment, and reduced staff turnover.

Application Activities

1. Conduct additional research on the Internet to learn more about the T.E.A.C.H. and WAGE$ programs. Use Application Worksheet 1-1 to develop an informational flier describing one of the programs.

2. Locate the NAEYC Code of Ethical Conduct on the organization's Web site (www.naeyc.org). Read *Section III. Ethical responsibilities to colleagues.* Identify three key issues addressed in this section that could be used for a staff training session, and record them on Application Worksheet 1-2. For each issue, list some key points to be discussed.

3. Compile a list of stress-relieving activities that you personally would find helpful, and record them on Application Worksheet 1-3. Select three activities and develop a realistic

Application Worksheet 1-1

The program

The objective of the program

Is this program available throughout the United States? Is it available in this state?

What eligibility requirements must be met to qualify?

Contact information for this state

What are the main points to identify about this program?

Application Worksheet 1-2

Why did NAEYC develop the Code of Ethical Conduct?

How can it be used in professional practice?

Ethical issues to address for staff training

A.

B.

C.

Key points to discuss about each issue

Ethical issue A:

Ethical issue B:

Ethical issue C:

Go to the NAEYC Web site (www.naeyc.org) and type "case studies" into the Search function. There you will find references to a number of case studies that demonstrate how the Code of Ethical Conduct can be used to address difficult decisions. Select one case study for a professional development activity with your staff.

▨ What ethical dilemma does the case study address?

▨ Have staff members work in pairs to identify the standards that could be used to resolve the ethical problem. Discuss the resolution as a group.

Application Worksheet 1-3

The most interesting and achievable stress-relieving activities

Three realistic stress-relieving goals

   a.

   b.

   c.

What obstacles are most likely to interfere with you achieving the above goals?

What steps can you take now to improve your chances of success?

Go to the Web site www.mypyramid.gov and click on "My Pyramid Tracker." Use this site to assess your dietary intake and physical activity levels for one week. What improvements could you make in these areas to improve your ability to handle stress?

goal for each (e.g., I will walk at least 30 minutes three days per week; I will eat more servings of fruits and vegetables each day; I will enroll in the painting class I've always wanted to take).

4. Interview eight early education teachers about their current level of job satisfaction. Find out what workplace conditions they find most frustrating or stressful. Prepare a graph illustrating your findings.

5. Develop a solution for each of the problems or conditions the teachers in Activity 4 identified. Present your ideas to the class or to your team, and have them critique each solution.

Discussion Points

1. What is stress? Discuss why some stress may actually be beneficial.

2. Explain why two teachers in the same classroom might react differently to the same stressful event.

3. A colleague confides in you that he no longer enjoys his first teaching job in a small early childhood center. What may he be experiencing? What workplace conditions might be contributing to his feelings?

4. Why is it especially important to adopt a motivational leadership style in early education settings?

5. Discuss why it is important to acknowledge employee efforts and workplace contributions. What are the likely consequences of not doing so?

6. What measures can be taken to address the comfort and safety of adults in early education programs?

References

Bond, R., & Bunce, D. (2001). Job control mediates change in a work reorganization intervention for stress reduction. *Journal of Occupational Health & Psychology, 6* (4), 290–302.

Bright, K. A., & Calabro, K. (1999). Child care workers and workplace hazards in the United States: Overview of research and implications for occupational health professionals. *Occupational Medicine* (London), *49*(7), 427–437.

Bureau of Labor Statistics. (2005). *Employment characteristics of families summary*. Washington, DC: U.S. Department of Labor. Retrieved September 15, 2005, from http://www.bls.gov/oco/cg/cgs032.htm.

Bureau of Labor Statistics. (2005). *Occupational outlook handbook, 2004–05 Edition, childcare workers*. Washington, DC: U.S. Department of Labor. Retrieved on September 20, 2005, from http://www.bls.gov/oco/cg/cgs032.htm.

Bureau of Labor Statistics. (2004). *20 Leading occupations of employed women full-time wage and salary workers, 2004 annual averages*. Washington, DC: Women's Bureau, U.S. Department of Labor. Retrieved September 20, 2005, from http://www.dol.gov/wb/factsheets/20lead2004.htm.

Center for the Child Care Workforce. (2004). *Current data on the salaries and benefits of the U.S. early childhood education workforce*. Washington, DC: Author.

Curbow, B., Spratt, K., Ungaretti, A., McDonnell, K., & Breckler, S. (2000). What makes some employees more resistant to burnout? *Early Childhood Research Quarterly, 15*(4), 515–536.

Helburn, S. W., & Howes, C. (1996). Child care cost and quality. *Future of Children, 6*(2), 62–82.

Jamison, C., Wallace, M., & Jamison, P. J. (2004). Contemporary work characteristics, stress, and ill health. *American Journal of Human Biology, 16*(1), 43–56.

Lamb, M. (2000). The effects of quality care on child development. *Applied Developmental Science, 4*(3), 112–115.

Liston, D. (2004). The lure of learning in teaching. *Teachers College Record, 106*(3), 459–486.

Murphy, L. (1996). Stress management in work settings: A critical review of the health effects. *American Journal of Health Promotion, 11*(2), 112–135.

National Association for the Education of Young Children (NAEYC). (2005). *Code of Ethical Conduct and Statement of Commitment*. Washington, DC: NAEYC. Retrieved December 4, 2005, from http://www.naeyc.org.

National Research Council and Institute of Medicine. (2000). *From neurons to neighborhoods: The science of early childhood development*. Jack P. Shonkoff & Deborah A. Phillips (Eds.). Washington, DC: National Academy Press.

National Institute of Child Health and Human Development Early Child Care Research Network (NICHD). (1998). *The NICHD study of early child care and youth development*. Retrieved on May 23, 2006, from http://secc.rti.org.

NICHD Early Child Care Research Network. (2000). The relation of child care to cognitive and language development. *Child Development, 71,* 960–980.

Papanastasiou, C., & Papanastasiou, E. (1997). Factors that influence students to become teachers. *Educational Research and Evaluation, 3* (4), 305–316.

Rushton, S. P. (2001). Applying brain research to create developmentally appropriate learning environments. *Young Children, 56* (5), 76–82.

Saluja, G., Early, D., & Clifford, R. (2002). Demographic characteristics of early childhood teachers and structural elements of early care and education in the United States. *Early Childhood Research & Practice, 4* (1). (Available online at http://ecrp.uiuc.edu/.)

Schaubroeck, J., & Fink, L. (1999). Facilitating and inhibiting effects of job control and social support on stress outcomes and role behavior: A contingency model. *Journal of Organizational Behavior, 19* (2), 167–195.

Schore, A. N. (2001). Effects of a secure attachment relationship on right brain development, affect regulation, and infant mental health. *Infant Mental Health Journal, 22* (1–2), 7–66.

Snow, C., Teleki, J., & Reguero-de-Atiles, J. (1996). Child care center licensing standards in the United States, 1981–1995. Public policy report. *Young Children, 51* (6), 36–41.

Whitebrook, M., Phillips, D., & Howes, M. (1993). *National child care staffing study revisited: Four years in the life of center-based child care.* Oakland, CA: The Child Care Employee Project.

Web Resources

Healthy Child Care America	*www.healthychildcare.org*
National Association for the Education of Young Children	*www.naeyc.org*
National Association of Child Care Resource and Referral Agencies	*www.naccrra.org*
National Resource Center for Health and Safety in Child Care	*http://nrc.uchsc.edu*
Occupational Safety and Health	*www.osha.org*

Chapter 2

What We Know about the Role of Motivation in Programs

Objectives

After reading this chapter, you will be able to:

- define the term *motivation*.
- discuss several factors that shape what motivates an individual.
- discuss the differences between intrinsic and extrinsic motivators.
- compare and contrast the motivational theories of Maslow, Herzberg, and McClelland.
- discuss why motivation is an important consideration in the workplace.
- identify the positive outcomes of effective employee motivation.

Key Terms

- environment
- extrinsic motivators
- hygienes
- intrinsic motivators
- motivation
- physiological needs
- regression
- self-actualization

> *"Outstanding leaders go out of their way to boost the self-esteem of their personnel. If people believe in themselves, it's amazing what they can accomplish."*
>
> SAM WALTON
> FOUNDER, WAL-MART

 ## Introduction

How often have you made decisions and later questioned why you made the choices you did? For example, why did you agree to work on your afternoon off when you already had other plans? What made you purchase a shirt just because it was on sale, although you really don't like the color blue? Why did you decide to return to school? What made you accept your current job?

Our motivations influence our decisions and actions, give us direction and purpose, maintain our interest, and energize us to begin a new project or continue in the face of adversity. In some instances, we can identify the things that motivate our behaviors, but not always. We may know that completing a degree is likely to help us land a better-paying job, but may not understand why we became short-tempered with a parent or colleague this afternoon.

 ## What Is Motivation?

Behavior is an intriguing phenomenon that is driven primarily by **motivation.** Our decisions, choices, and actions are continuously influenced by a complex system of human needs. Efforts to satisfy these needs cause us to behave in specific ways. And, once a need is satisfied, it loses its motivating power. Some needs, such as thirst and hunger, are common to everyone, while others, such as the needs for affection, recognition, and self-esteem, are of a higher order and, therefore, unique to an individual. Differences in biological makeup, culture, **environment,** and lifelong experiences collectively influence and shape the things each of us finds personally motivating (Figure 2-1). Consequently, things that motivate one employee may not prove to be motivating to another. Also, things that an employee finds motivating today may not be as

Figure 2-1   Individual differences influence what we find personally motivating.

fulfilling a year from now. In some instances, we are able to recognize these powerful emotions for what they are and understand how they affect our behavior—but this is not always the case.

Connecting Points: You have a big psychology exam scheduled on Monday, but your friends call and invite you to spend the weekend at the lake. You know that you really need to study in order to improve your final grade in this class from a B+ to an A.

- Identify all of the motivating factors in this situation.
- What effect is each factor likely to produce?
- How is the outcome likely to differ depending on your decision?
- Which motivating factor would you be most likely to choose, and why?

 ## When Is Motivation Important?

Motivation explains why we find certain opportunities attractive and dedicate time and energy to pursue them. How valuable or invaluable an individual perceives an experience to be, or not to be, ultimately influences the direction of his or her behavior. For example, what makes some employees volunteer to assist with a weekend fund-raising event when they won't be paid for the time they donate? Why are parents willing to make cookies for the school's annual bake sale? Or, why isn't an assistant teacher interested in applying for the lead teacher opening? In each case, these individuals were motivated by something they found personally rewarding.

The concept of motivation is also useful for understanding the amount of effort a person is willing to invest to accomplish a goal. For example, what makes one teacher perform above and beyond the requirements of the position description, while another simply does what is necessary to get by? Why does the same teacher volunteer whenever the director needs help with a special project, while other teachers must be asked? What we do know is that when employees experience pleasure and satisfaction in their work, the quantity and quality of their effort typically increase until their needs are meet. The opposite is also true. A decline in a teacher's performance and productivity may indicate a lack of interest and personal fulfillment.

An individual's willingness to persist at a given task is also influenced by the degree of motivation. For example, a few words of encouragement can be energizing and make a teacher feel that her or his efforts are appreciated: "I know the children are really going to enjoy the new science center you have planned." When employees believe that no one cares or feel that their needs are not adequately met, they soon lose interest in their work and often leave. The leader who builds challenge, opportunity, and recognition into work activities increases the likelihood of retaining employees who are also committed to their jobs.

Retention of dedicated employees is the number one concern of leaders in any business or organization. This is an especially critical issue in the field of early childhood education, which typically experiences an annual turnover rate higher than 30 percent (Center for the Child Care Workforce, 2004). Because motivation plays a key role in the retention process, it is important that leaders understand the basic principles of motivation and how to put them into practice (Figure 2-2). Motivation exerts a direct influence on employees' interests, efforts, and persistence in accomplishing an organization's goals and objectives. However, determining what motivates individual employees and how to create workplace environments that encourage optimum performance can present a major leadership challenge.

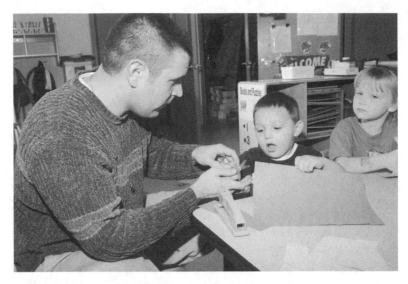

Figure 2-2 Motivation plays a critical role in retaining employees.

The Director's Showcase

What motivational strategies have you found effective in boosting staff morale?

"Getting to know staff is critical—identifying their strengths and then finding ways to use them is especially motivating. We also find multiple ways (nonmonetary) to surprise and recognize employees' contributions, which boosts their self-esteem and morale."

Diane Schultz, Director
Family Services
BryanLGH Medical Center
Lincoln, NE

Theoretical Models of Motivation

Several classical theories have been proposed to improve our understanding of human motivational needs and how they can be satisfied in the workplace. It is unlikely that any particular theory provides a completely satisfactory explanation. However, elements from each of these theories can be useful for understanding the concept of motivation. Persons in leadership positions can use elements from theoretical frameworks to better understand their employees' needs and to design reward systems that are individualized, efficient, and effective motivators.

Maslow's Needs Hierarchy

Abraham Maslow, a noted psychologist, was intrigued by what motivated people to act on a real or perceived need or task. Why, for example, do some individuals seek employment while others don't? What causes some early childhood teachers to leave an organization while others remain for years? Why do people seek out friends and desire companionship? Why do some teachers seem to be more productive than others?

Maslow (1968) described five categories of basic human needs based on his observations. These categories are typically represented in a triangular model, commonly called Maslow's hierarchy of needs, and arranged in ascending order, from needs he considered to be the most essential and life-sustaining to those of the highest intellectual order (Figure 2-3):

■ **physiological needs**—requirements necessary to sustain life, including food, water, shelter, and air

■ physical and psychological safety—feelings of safety, security, and freedom from harm in one's environment

■ belongingness—the drive for social connection, friendships, acceptance, love, and group membership

■ self-esteem—an internal need to achieve respect, establish a positive reputation, and feel appreciated by others

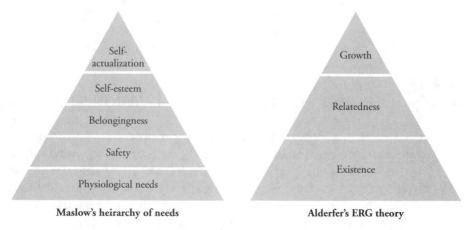

Maslow's heirarchy of needs   Alderfer's ERG theory

Figure 2-3   A comparison of Maslow's and Alderfer's needs theories.

■ **self-actualization**—the feeling of personal satisfaction derived from utilizing one's talents and potential to achieve independent thinking, creative expression, and problem solving

Maslow's theories provided a valuable starting point for understanding what motivates individual behavior. He assumed that everyone is motivated by the same basic needs and that people have needs in multiple areas. His ideas also acknowledged a person's desire for personal and professional growth, a concept that has important implications for early education programs in terms of providing professional staff-development opportunities. However, Maslow's ideas have been criticized for overgeneralizing the motivational process. His theory fails to acknowledge individual differences in motivational preferences and the ways in which needs are satisfied. Maslow also believed that people's needs had to be completely satisfied at each level before they were able to progress to the next higher level, and that upward movement could be achieved only in a stepwise manner. Some psychologists have suggested that Maslow's ideas are not supported with sound research, and that his interpretations of human behavior may not be entirely correct (Heylighten, 1992; Wahba & Bridwell, 1976). However, his theory remains an important contribution to our understanding of human motivational needs.

ERG Theory

Clayton Alderfer saw merit in Maslow's ideas and attempted to address criticism of the hierarchy of needs theory by simplifying his concepts. Alderfer (1972) proposed the ERG theory, which recognizes three basic motivational needs he believed all humans share (Figure 2-3):

■ existence—physiological and safety needs; combines Maslow's physiological and safety categories

■ relatedness—an individual's need to form social relationships and communicate with other people; is similar to Maslow's belongingness category

■ growth—an internal drive for personal achievement, peer recognition, and lifelong interest in learning; combines Maslow's self-esteem and self-actualization categories

The ERG theory differs on several fundamental points from Maslow's ideas on motivation. Alderfer believed that:

■ individuals have different needs: not everyone is motivated by the same things.

- needs can be satisfied on multiple levels simultaneously.

- needs do not have to be entirely satisfied on one level before an individual can begin addressing motivational needs on a higher level.

- it isn't necessary to satisfy motivational needs in any particular order.

- frustration and **regression** play an important role in need satisfaction.

Alderfer suggested that when individuals experience frustration in attempting to satisfy higher-level needs, they often regress to a comfort level where their needs are currently being met. For example, an employee who is in line for a promotion (Growth) but doesn't receive it may devote more time and energy to socializing with colleagues (Relatedness). Or, a teacher who is assigned to a classroom that she hadn't requested (Relatedness) may find a salary increase (Existence) more personally motivating. Temporary regression can have a number of positive outcomes for individuals by giving them additional time to acquire new skills, build confidence, or rethink their strategies.

Herzberg's Two-Factor Theory

Frederick Herzberg's ideas also shed light on the role of motivation in the workplace (Herzberg, Mausner, & Snyderman, 1959). After surveying hundreds of employees, he concluded that motivation is determined by two factors.

- motivators—opportunities that foster an employee's personal sense of job satisfaction, such as formal recognition, assignment of new responsibilities, and promotions (Figure 2-4)

- **hygienes**—working conditions, such as the physical setting, relationships with colleagues and supervisors, and company policies that can influence an employee's sense of job satisfaction or dissatisfaction

Herzberg believed that motivators and hygienes function relatively independently of each other. For example, painting the break room (hygienes) isn't likely to have much effect on improving teachers' motivation, performance, or job satisfaction, although teachers may appreciate the effort. In contrast, an assistant teacher who is promoted to a lead position (motivator) in the same classroom may feel a sense of renewed commitment.

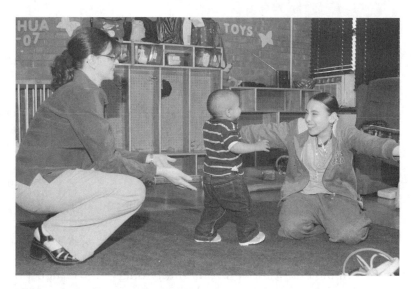

Figure 2-4 Personally fulfilling work serves as a powerful motivator.

Although Herzberg's ideas have been criticized for overlooking the effect working conditions can have on employee attitude and performance, his theories have drawn positive attention to the idea that a person's job responsibilities may serve as significant motivators in and by themselves. When employees believe their work or role is personally fulfilling, the job itself becomes an important motivator. This insight suggests that leaders should look for ways to add interest, pizzazz, and challenge to an employee's position, and to adopt a leadership style that acknowledges employees' contributions on a regular basis.

Connecting Points: As the director of Wee Kids Early Education Center, you would like to give every staff member a small raise this year. However, after reviewing the annual budget, you realize this isn't possible. Should you just forget about trying to reward your employees for now?

- What no-cost hygienes might you provide instead of a raise?
- Do you think your employees will find these motivators as rewarding as a salary increase?
- What advantages do hygienes offer?

McClelland's Theory of Learned Needs

David McClelland was also interested in Maslow's categorization of motivational needs. He conducted experimental studies to understand better the origin of such needs and how they might ultimately influence an individual's behavior. Based on this work, McClelland proposed three major categories that he believed serve as human motivators: the needs for power, achievement, and affiliation (McClelland & Burnham, 1976).

The Need for Power.   McClelland believed the quest for power serves as a primary motivating factor for individuals who assume leadership positions. He suggested that status, social recognition, and influence over others satisfy a fundamental human need for self-fulfillment. Although some individuals utilize their position for personal gain and career advancement, others are committed to achieving their organization's goals. McClelland also argued that these same qualities are necessary for one to be an effective leader, and that leaders are morally obligated to perform their duties in an ethical manner.

The Need for Achievement.   McClelland observed that some individuals appear to seek out, and thrive on, challenge. He described this group as having a strong motivational need for achievement; they typically exhibit a high level of personal energy, initiative, and persistence in their work. McClelland also noted their preference for assuming responsibility, taking on leadership positions, engaging in problem-solving activities, and requesting feedback in order to improve their performance and success. Although these individuals possess many positive characteristics, McClelland observed that high achievers are often reluctant to delegate tasks to other workers, preferring instead to maintain control of decisions and outcomes. When work or work environments no longer provide adequate challenge, these individuals are likely to leave.

The Need for Affiliation.   McClelland recognized that some individuals have an intense need for social interaction and close social relationships with others (Figure 2-5). He noted that these individuals prefer to work cooperatively in teams or groups, engage in social activities, conform, seek out approval, and be liked by others. They typically avoid positions that require assertiveness, initiative, independent decision making, or major supervisory responsibility.

Figure 2-5 Some employees have a strong need to socialize.

McClelland suggested that individuals with a high need for affiliation do not make effective leaders or supervisors because they find it difficult to give critical feedback, often show favoritism, and are reluctant to enforce rules or policy (McClelland & Burnham, 1976).

McClelland thought that all these need behaviors are learned as the result of socialization and reinforcement through parental influence, cultural values, and individual personality. His ideas help us to understand that individual employees have needs that may be quite different from one another. Leaders who appreciate and are sensitive to these differences can use them to create teams that are effective and able to work together.

The Director's Showcase

What do you think healthy employee morale should look like in your program?

"Healthy employee morale is evident when there is an environment of mutual trust and open communication, cooperation, the staff feels empowered, the center's mission and vision are accomplished through team work, and staff members have fun working together."

Candy Seltman, Administrative Director
Shawnee Mission Medical Center Child
Care Center
Shawnee Mission, KS

The Expectancy Theory

The expectancy theory suggests that people expect to be rewarded appropriately for their efforts (Vroom, 1964). Three conditions are implied:

- whether individuals believe the effort invested will pay off or enable them to accomplish a given task—for example, "If I devote more time to preparing lesson plans, my day will run more smoothly."
- whether individuals believe that good performance will be rewarded—for example, "My supervisor will notice how efficiently I am running my classroom, and consider giving me a raise."
- how personally satisfying (or not satisfying) individuals find a reward that acknowledges their effort—for example, "My director brought in brownies today to celebrate my one-year anniversary as a teacher with this program. She knows I can't eat chocolate."

Leaders will find this theory particularly helpful in understanding the connections among employee performance, motivation, and retention. When employees believe their efforts are sincerely appreciated, they tend to work even harder. Teachers are a prime example. Most would agree that it is the children, not their paycheck, that motivates teachers to devote as much time and energy to their jobs as they do. On the other hand, when employees no longer feel their efforts are being acknowledged, or that opportunity is lacking, they may begin to lose interest, perform poorly, and eventually leave their job.

Also implied in this theory is the idea that individuals will be able to identify and express what they find rewarding. However, people don't always know what motivates them. Successful leaders can utilize a variety of effective strategies, such as holding individual or group discussions, providing self-evaluation tools, or inviting motivational speakers, to help employees explore the types of motivators they might find personally satisfying (see Appendix B for additional resources).

Equity Theory

Employees expect to be treated fairly and equitably for their contributions. No employee wants to feel that an organization or leader is taking advantage of his or her time, skills, or efforts. However, how just or fair an employee considers the amount and distribution of rewards can have either a positive or a negative effect on behavior. For example, a teacher who believes she deserves the "teacher of the month" award, but is passed over, may feel resentment toward her colleagues. On the other hand, an assistant teacher who is promoted to a lead position is likely to experience a boost in self-esteem and confidence.

The equity theory recognizes these fundamental human precepts (Adams, 1963). It acknowledges that employees expect their rewards to be not only fair but also comparable to what their colleagues are receiving for similar work (Figure 2-6). If employees think, or discover, that they are not receiving equivalent compensation or acknowledgement, they may convey their resentment in a variety of ways. For example, if I find out that my raise is half of what my co-teacher received, I may consider quitting, calling in sick more often, taking home "extra" office supplies, or not volunteering for special center events. On the other hand, if I've received a larger pay raise than other teachers, it may motivate me to work even harder or offer to take on extra projects.

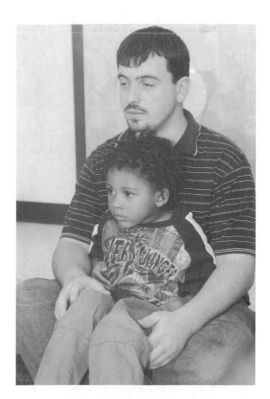

Figure 2-6 Employees expect to be rewarded fairly for their efforts.

Because an employee's interpretation of fairness and equity is influenced by personal values, belief systems, and access to information, leaders are continuously challenged to be sure they are rewarding employees in a way that is consistent and fair to everyone. Getting to know your employees, documenting their contributions and efforts, understanding how various incentives are likely to affect their behavior, and avoiding favoritism can avoid many unhappy experiences.

What Are Intrinsic and Extrinsic Rewards?

DeCharms (1968) offered yet another explanation for how motivation influences employee performance. He described motivators as being either extrinsic or intrinsic based on their primary origination. Examples of **extrinsic motivators** include a pay raise, assignment to a better office space, a new job title, a prize, or an extra day off. They are tangible rewards offered by another individual in acknowledgement of an employee's performance. **Intrinsic motivators** are derived from an internal or personal sense of accomplishment, and include feelings such as excitement, increased interest or energy, enjoyment, and pleasure. Consider, for example, how exciting it is to watch a toddler take his first steps or a child write her name for the first time, or the feeling of pride when a coworker offers a compliment!

Extrinsic and intrinsic motivators each have their own distinct advantages and disadvantages. Researchers have determined that employees who have only limited control over their jobs or few opportunities for creative input are more likely to respond to extrinsic rewards (Eisenberger, Rhoades, & Cameron, 1999). They simply perform their work and then expect to be compensated in some manner. Extrinsic motivators can have a positive initial effect on employee behavior, but the effect is often short-lived. After the reward exhilaration passes, employees resume their normal efforts. Consider, for example, how rewarding you would still find the 25-cent-an-hour raise you received six months ago on a day when three of your teachers just called in sick!

Intrinsic rewards, on the other hand, generally have a more lasting effect on employee performance and commitment. Teachers who enjoy greater freedom and control in their job are more likely to be motivated by rewards that contribute to their personal feelings of satisfaction and accomplishment. However, as we have seen, individuals are seldom motivated by a single factor. Effective leaders must be sensitive to employees' individual needs and utilize a variety of motivating strategies to ensure long-term commitment and optimum performance.

What Role Does Motivation Play in the Early Childhood Workplace?

Motivation is clearly important to a program's success (Figure 2-7). It can increase recruitment success, improve retention rates, help assure high staff productivity, and boost morale. The opposite is also true. Programs that fail to create a positive work environment or to address their employees' needs are unlikely to experience lasting success.

Working conditions in the field of early education make it especially important to adopt a motivational leadership style (Pacini, 2000). Limited resources, challenging diversity issues, social changes, long hours, and demanding work have led to consistently high turnover rates. Numerous studies have documented a strong relationship between employee motivation and retention rates (Levine, 2001; Whitebrook & Bellm, 1999; Whitebrook & Sakai, 2003). The

Figure 2-7 Mentoring and motivating employees are essential leadership roles.

degree of motivation an employee perceives in his or her job can have a positive or negative effect on attendance, performance, morale, self-esteem, personal interest, and professional growth (Bandura, 1997; Harrison & Martocchio, 1998). When teachers feel valued and respected, they are more likely to remain in their positions, whereas employees who feel unappreciated tend to leave sooner. Supportive workplace environments can also have a positive effect on a program's recruiting efforts and other substantial returns for the organization.

Productivity is also directly influenced by the motivational climate established in the workplace. Teachers may possess all of the required skills and experience, but it is upto leaders to create an atmosphere that encourages individuals to utilize their full potentials. Leaders must be willing to invest time and effort in building a positive motivational environment and to respect their staff as individuals—to know their personal interests, preferences, needs, and values—in order to provide reinforcers that are meaningful (Moline, 2005). This process must be ongoing because circumstances and teachers' needs are continuously changing. Motivational leaders who are sensitive to these changes are able to create challenging, rewarding workplace environments. They can also empower employees to assume responsibility, develop new skills, make decisions, become independent thinkers, and assume leadership roles.

Summary

- Several classical theories have proven helpful for understanding human motivational needs and how they can be satisfied in the workplace.

- Maslow's hierarchy of needs theory identifies five levels of fundamental needs: physiological, safety, belongingness, esteem, and self-actualization.

- The ERG theory groups human motivational needs into three categories.
    - Existence—essential physiological and safety needs
    - Relatedness—the need for social interaction and relationships
    - Growth—the internal drive to achieve positive self-esteem and recognition

- Herzberg described two basic categories of motivators: those associated with one's job responsibilities and those related to working conditions (e.g., policies, facilities).

- McClelland attributed motivation to the satisfaction of human desires for achievement, affiliation, and power or control. He believed these needs are learned through experience and socialization.

- Expectancy theory acknowledges that people expect their efforts to be recognized and rewarded; when this is lacking, people develop apathy toward their work.

- Equity theory recognizes that employees expect to be treated fairly.

- Motivators can be either intrinsic or extrinsic. Extrinsic motivators are external rewards. Intrinsic rewards create an internal sense of satisfaction or pleasure. Employees must have both their intrinsic and extrinsic needs met to remain motivated.

Application Activities

1. Develop a questionnaire, based on the theories described in this chapter, that could be used to assess an employee's level of motivation. Write your questionnaire on Application Worksheet 2-1.

2. Conduct an online search for Web sites that address the concept of motivational leadership. Select five of the most useful sites. On Application Worksheet 2-2, write a brief summary describing the type of information and resources provided.

3. Interview the administrators of two different early education programs. Ask them to describe what they do to motivate staff members. Evaluate the effectiveness of their motivational incentives and practices based on what you've learned in this chapter. Record your interview and assessment on Application Worksheet 2-3.

4. Develop a list of incentives that would motivate you to improve your eating or exercise habits. Record your list on Application Worksheet 2-4.

Application Worksheet 2-1

Prepare a list of questions that will be effective for assessing an employee's level of motivation. Provide a brief rationale (based on the theories described in this chapter) for why you included each question.

Discuss how leaders could use the information from this questionnaire for motivational purposes.

Application Worksheet 2-2

List the sites you found most informative for understanding the concept of motivational leadership (include the Web site address and a summary description of each site).

A.

B.

C.

D.

E.

Others:

Application Worksheet 2-3

After interviewing two directors, record the motivational strategies/ practices they commonly use to acknowledge employees' performance. Next, critique each of the strategies, based on the information presented in this chapter, on its potential effectiveness. List advantages and disadvantages. What alternative motivators would you recommend?

Motivational strategies used by Director A

Motivational strategies used by Director B

Application Worksheet 2-4

List the incentives that would motivate you to improve your eating or exercise habits.

What motivational needs does each incentive meet (based on the theories presented in this chapter)?

How effective do you think each incentive would be in helping you make changes in your diet or physical activity?

What could you do to increase the motivational value of these incentives?

Discussion Points

1. What short- and long-term effects is a 10-cent-an-hour raise likely to have on employee motivation?

2. Should all employees who perform similar jobs be rewarded equally?

3. Have you ever participated in a group project and felt that you were not rewarded fairly for your contributions? Use the equity theory to explain why you might feel this way.

4. How can a leader use the need for affiliation to build effective team relationships?

5. Examine several of the personal and professional decisions you've made recently. What needs do you think your choices satisfied?

6. Person X is running for mayor of your hometown. His campaign ads air nightly on the local TV station, he is frequently invited to speaking engagements, and he appears at numerous public events. After losing the election, he removes himself from all political activities and resumes his office job. How would Alderfer explain this change?

References

Adams, J. (1963). Toward an understanding of inequity. *Journal of Abnormal Psychology, 67,* 422–436.

Alderfer, C. P. (1972). *Existence, relatedness, and growth: Human needs in organizational settings.* New York: Free Press.

Bandura, A. (1997). *Self-efficacy: The exercise of control.* New York: W. H. Freeman.

Center for the Child Care Workforce. (2004). *Current data on the salaries and benefits of the U.S. early childhood education workforce.* Washington, DC: Author.

deCharms, R. (1968). *Personal causation: The internal affective determinants of behavior.* New York: Academic Press.

Eisenberger, R., Rhoades, L., & Cameron, J. (1999). Does pay for performance increase or decrease perceived self-determination and intrinsic motivation? *Journal of Personality and Social Psychology, 177,* 1026–1040.

Harrison, D. A., & Martocchio, J. J. (1998). Time for absenteeism: A 20-year review of origins, offshoots, and outcomes. *Journal of Management, 24,* 305–350.

Herzberg, F., Mausner, B., & Snyderman, B. (1959). *The motivation to work.* New York: John Wiley.

Heylighten, F. (1992). A cognitive systematic reconstruction of Maslow's theory of self-actualization. *Behavioral Science, 37,* 39–58.

Levine, L. (2001). *The child care workforce.* Washington, DC: Congressional Research Services.

Maslow, A. (1968). *Toward a psychology of being* (2nd ed.). New York: Van Nostrand Reinhold Company.

McClelland, D. C., & Burnham, D. H. (1976). Power is the great motivator. *Harvard Business Review, 54* (2), 100–110.

Moline, L. A. (2005). Unlocking the potential of your employees: The not-so-secret secrets of motivational leadership. *Government Finance Review, 21* (1), 12–16.

Pacini, L. A. (2000). The power of empowerment. *Young Children, 55* (6), 83–85.

Vroom, V. H. (1964). *Work and motivation.* New York: John Wiley.

Wahba, M., & Bridwell, L. (1976). Maslow reconsidered: A review of research on the need theory. *Organizational Behavior and Human Performance, 15,* 212–240.

Whitebrook, M., & Bellm, D. (1999). *Taking on turnover: An action guide for child care center teachers and directors.* Washington, DC: Center for the Child Care Workforce.

Whitebrook, M., & Sakai, L. (2003). Turnover begets turnover: An examination of job and occupational instability among child care center staff. *Early Childhood Research Quarterly, 18* (3), 273–293.

Web Resources

Employer-Employee.com	*www.employer-employee.com*
GovLeaders.org	*www.govleaders.org*
Mind Tools (leadership and motivation)	*www.mindtools.com*
Small business know-how	*www.businessknowhow.com*
Workforce management	*www.workforce.com*

Chapter 3

The Motivational Leader

Objectives

After reading this chapter, you will be able to:

- discuss how individuals typically become leaders in organizations.
- describe several key functions that leaders are expected to perform.
- compare and contrast the autocratic and participative leadership styles, including the advantages and limitations of each.
- distinguish between transactional and transformational leadership.
- describe how an ordinary leader can become a motivational leader.

Key Terms

- attributes
- autocratic
- consultative
- definitive
- laissez–faire

- participative
- punitive
- traits
- transactional
- transformational

> *"Example is not the main thing in influencing others.
> It is the only thing."*
>
> Dr. Albert Schweitzer

 ## Introduction

The leadership concept is the subject of this chapter, but before we turn our attention to the topic, we want to emphasize that whenever the terms *leader* and *leadership* are mentioned in this book, their use is not limited to an individual who holds a formal title or sits in a designated office. Motivational leaders are found throughout an organization (Figure 3-1). They have many different titles, including office managers, head teachers, directors, team leaders, and program coordinators. In other words, anyone who makes decisions, mentors, or encourages another employee's performance is displaying leadership qualities.

Figure 3-1 Motivational leaders are found throughout an organization.

In Chapters 1 and 2, we discussed a number of key motivational theories and employee needs in the workplace. Now, we will turn our attention to the individuals who occupy leadership positions, and focus on their personal qualifications, roles and responsibilities, and leadership styles. Finally, we will discuss practices that will help you become an exemplary motivational leader.

 ## Motivational Leadership

Few individuals receive any formal leadership training, yet many persons find themselves in leadership positions for reasons that are unrelated to their qualifications for the job. This pattern is especially true in early childhood programs (Bloom, 1997). Some people become leaders because they have worked for an organization the longest or because no one else wants to assume the responsibility of a leadership role. Others may actively seek leadership positions because they enjoy the recognition or a formal title. Still other individuals may have won their colleagues' respect and admiration because they have demonstrated their leadership abilities, or they may have a sincere interest in contributing to their organization.

Regardless of the path that has led an individual to a leadership position, it is performance that truly matters. A program's success or failure ultimately depends on the quality of its leadership because motivational leaders set the tone for an organization through their ability to influence almost every function, including:

- the decision-making process.
- the use of power and authority.
- resource allocation.
- program stability.
- employee behavior and performance.
- conflict resolution.
- customer satisfaction.

Effective leadership enables an organization to run smoothly and to accomplish its goals and objectives. In contrast, poor leadership can contribute to organizational inefficiency, confusion, unhappy employees, loss of consumers, and eventual failure.

Motivational leaders play a key role in assuring program success because they understand the "big picture" and are not likely to get bogged down by small problems and minute details. They must be able to assess situations efficiently, formulate responsive plans, and rally the resources necessary to achieve an objective. They must build trust and loyalty among employees through their support, guidance, and inspiration. In other words, organizations rely on motivational leaders to make sound decisions, establish and maintain open lines of communication with employees, and achieve an organization's goals and mission.

The leadership role has been the subject of numerous studies, yet many questions remain unanswered. For example, is there a specific path one can follow to become a leader? Are people born to be leaders, or do they acquire leadership skills through training and experience? Which leadership style is most effective? Should a leader be people or outcome oriented? Is it more productive to share leadership responsibilities, or should one person be solely in charge? A clearer understanding about the effects and importance of motivational leadership for an organization and its employees continues to evolve as answers to some of these questions become apparent.

The Director's Showcase

What motivational challenges are you currently facing in your program?

"Since I am relatively new to this program, I believe building trust with my teachers is most important. I want them to know that I have their interests at heart and am always looking out for them. I am also still trying to learn what motivates individual staff members because I think it is critical to successful motivation."

Michelle Scott
Early Education Program Director
Ballard Community Center, Lawrence, KS

Personal Leadership Qualities

For decades, researchers were intrigued by the possibility that outstanding leaders possessed certain exceptional **traits** that distinguished them from nonleaders (Figure 3-2). They believed these

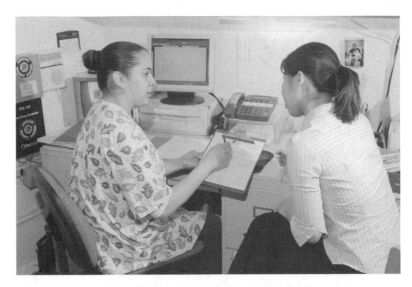

Figure 3-2   What special qualities do effective leaders possess?

inborn qualities were unique to certain individuals and thus responsible for their leadership success (Mann, 1959; Stogdill, 1948). Researchers began to study a variety of characteristics, such as height, weight, eye color, intelligence, attractiveness, ethnicity, gender, age, political orientation, religious affiliation, personality, popularity, and socioeconomic status, in an attempt to determine whether any traits could predict leadership capability. However, a **definitive** list of qualities that gifted leaders share has never been established, ending speculation that individuals are born with special leadership abilities.

Connecting Points: Leaders and teachers have many qualities in common. Children often think of their teachers as special people who seem to know everything about everything. Take a minute to recall your favorite teacher.

- Why do you consider this teacher special?
- What qualities do you find especially admirable about this teacher?
- Which of these qualities, if any, do you think would be important for a motivational leader to exhibit? Explain.
- Did this person exhibit any qualities that you feel would be inappropriate for a motivational leader to use in the workplace? Describe.

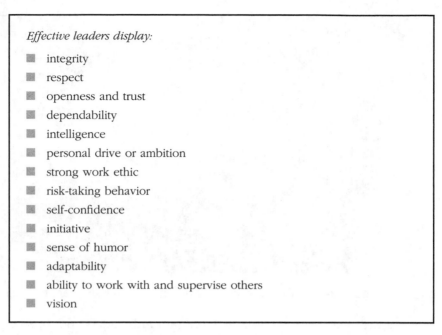

Effective leaders display:

- integrity
- respect
- openness and trust
- dependability
- intelligence
- personal drive or ambition
- strong work ethic
- risk-taking behavior
- self-confidence
- initiative
- sense of humor
- adaptability
- ability to work with and supervise others
- vision

Figure 3-3   Qualities of effective leaders.

Although clear evidence may be lacking, most people would agree that successful leaders tend to exhibit certain leadership **attributes** (Figure 3-3). Similar lists of these qualities appear in almost every book published on the topic of leadership. Although these lists are fairly consistent, differences may reflect the complex nature of the leadership role and diverse settings in which leaders typically function. Variations in program goals and objectives, the nature of employees (e.g., training, experience, values, personalities), and customers' needs and expectations require different combinations of leadership abilities (Gardner, 1989). However, it may also be true that leaders who possess different leadership traits are able to address similar problems, but in their own unique style.

 ## Leadership Roles

The quality of a program is often a direct reflection of its leadership. Leaders are expected to attract and retain dedicated employees. Programs also depend on leaders to keep their organizations running smoothly based on their ability to continually gather relevant information, maintain open lines of communication, and make critical decisions. They rely on leaders to recognize opportunity and to mobilize the resources necessary to move in new directions.

Because motivational leadership is fundamental to a program's success and vitality, researchers continue to examine the key roles that leaders are expected to perform. These responsibilities may include the ability to:

- organize
- facilitate
- communicate
- motivate
- mentor
- establish a vision
- build teams
- mediate
- delegate
- innovate
- be a role model

Such lists may be beneficial for identifying and evaluating persons being considered for leadership positions; however, individuals may not be proficient in all aspects of leadership, and this may not be necessary. In some instances, programs may purposely seek out individuals who have specific expertise to address current problems, achieve existing goals and objectives, or develop new initiatives.

It is generally assumed that leaders will be capable of performing routine responsibilities as well as respond to unexpected challenges (Figure 3-4). Thus, the greater their flexibility and repertoire of skills, the more likely they are to be successful. However, because leaders function at multiple levels within their organizations, it may not be necessary for every leader to possess the same level of expertise. Different situations—and continually changing circumstances—often require leaders to utilize different leadership skills. Leaders who lack expertise in certain leadership roles may develop new skills and improve their proficiency with time. They may also call upon other leaders within and outside of the organization who have talents in areas where they may not.

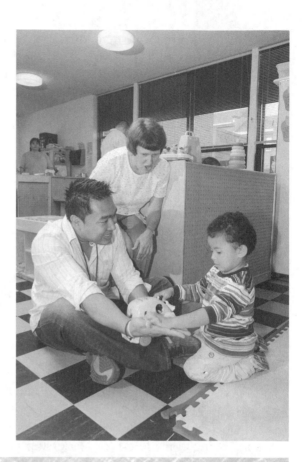

Figure 3-4
Successful leaders must be flexible and able to respond to the unexpected.

Connecting Points: Leader A is trying to organize a yearlong series of professional development training opportunities for the teachers in her center. Leader B is trying to work through a dispute between two of his classroom teachers.

■ What leadership skills does each of these leaders need to successfully fulfill their responsibilities?

■ How do these skills compare? How do they differ?

■ What options might Leader B consider if conflict resolution isn't one of his leadership strengths?

Some leaders also work more effectively to meet the needs of certain groups of employees. For example, a leader may have first-hand knowledge of specific classroom responsibilities and thus be able to relate more directly to her teachers' concerns about safety issues or staffing shortages. Other leaders have a better understanding of certain cultural values and are able to communicate and respond to employees' unique needs in a sensitive manner. Personality differences can also influence leadership effectiveness by enhancing or interfering with working relationships.

 ## Leadership Styles

The way in which an individual guides, shapes, and leads others toward an accomplishment or outcome is commonly referred to as *leadership style*. For decades, this topic has undergone extensive study and has been examined from a variety of perspectives, including the decision-making process, whether leaders show greater concern for outcomes or empowerment of their employees, and how resources are allocated (House & Aditya, 1997). The collective findings have contributed to an improved understanding of leadership and its effect on organizational success.

Decision Making and Control

One way to understand leadership style and how it influences an organization is to consider who controls the power and authority to make decisions, and how much support and involvement employees have in the process (Vroom, 1974). Four basic styles have been described:

- autocratic
- consultative
- participative
- laissez-faire

Leaders who practice an **autocratic** style maintain full personal control over all decision-making responsibilities. Employees are not consulted but are told how they are to perform a task, and then they are closely monitored as they work. The autocratic leader essentially sets policy and generates all ideas. There are no opportunities for constructive criticism by employees, either in the formulation of a task or in its completion. If the autocratic leader makes a mistake in defining a task or making an assignment, the employee is likely to experience any negative consequences. Although this leadership style limits employee input and creativity, there are times when it may be used appropriately in early childhood settings. For example, if you are working with newly hired

Figure 3-5 Leaders who practice a consultative style listen carefully to their employees.

teachers or staff whose skills and experience are limited, or you are trying to implement a new procedure, it is necessary to give instructions that are clear and explicit.

Leaders who practice a **consultative** style tend to listen attentively to employee suggestions and comments, but they always make the final decisions about what will be done, how it is to be completed, and who will be assigned to the task (Figure 3-5). The leader, in this case, also supervises employees' work closely. Again, there is essentially one person, the leader, who assumes responsibility for task formulation, assignment, and completion (Yukl, 1994). Although employees are encouraged to contribute their ideas, questions, and feedback, their actions don't necessarily translate into implementation.

The **participative** style reflects a teamwork approach and is generally considered more democratic than the other leadership styles. Employees are encouraged to participate in decision-making and problem-solving processes, typically in a group setting. This team approach is characterized by:

- considerable employee input and discussion.
- decisions that are reached collectively before they are presented to leadership.
- leadership that grants final approval.

Employees receive minimal instruction and are relatively free to determine how a task can best be accomplished to achieve a satisfactory outcome. For example, a participative approach is commonly used in early childhood programs when conducting IEP (individualized education plans) conferences or team meetings. This form of leadership is most effective with employees who are skilled and experienced; it builds self-confidence, self-esteem, professional growth, and future leadership skills.

Finally, the **laissez-faire** leadership style turns all decision-making responsibilities over to the employees. In this "hands-off" approach, decisions are reached and tasks performed with minimal to no direction or support from leadership. This style works well with highly skilled employees and takes advantage of their abilities and creativity. However, the lack of clear direction or a designated leader may result in confusion, disorganization, tasks that may not be completed as originally scheduled, and outcomes that differ from original expectations. Despite its potential limitations, the laissez-faire style can be effective in situations where leaders want to maximize employees' creativity and abilities. Brainstorming sessions, for example, encourage participants to express their ideas and concerns without constraint. Clear guidelines for responsibility must be established, however, or a leader may find that nothing concrete is accomplished despite good intentions.

The Director's Showcase

What motivational strategies have you found effective in boosting staff morale?

"I find that listening to teachers and implementing their suggestions whenever possible is very effective for boosting staff morale. I also encourage staff to serve on various committees in the center and hospital. Staff members also appreciate the gift certificates and special occasion treat events that acknowledge their individual and team efforts."

Candy Seltman
Administrative Director
Shawnee Mission Medical Center
Child Care Center
Shawnee Mission, KS

People versus Task Orientation

Leadership styles have also been studied from a behavioral perspective and characterized by the way in which leaders allocate their time, efforts, and resources (Blake & Mouton, 1964; Yukl, 1994). For example, some leaders adopt a task-oriented approach and then measure their personal success based on an organization's accomplishments. The task-oriented leader views employees as a means to an end (Figure 3-6). In other words, employees are assigned tasks, given directions, and expected to achieve predetermined goals according to the leader's standards. In contrast, people-oriented leaders tend to show a greater concern and respect for their employees as individuals. They are more likely to devote time and attention to building employee relationships than to attaining goals (Horner, 2003).

Most leaders are able to practice a style that falls somewhere between these two extremes, adjusting their approach and expectations to meet the demands of a particular situation. For example, an early childhood director who successfully recruits parents to help refurbish an outdoor play area may ask the group to choose their own project coordinator. This approach relieves the director of having to appoint a leader and taking the risk of hurting anyone's feelings, yet assures that someone will be accountable for overseeing the project.

Figure 3-6 Task-oriented leaders set goals and depend on their employees to achieve them.

Transactional and Transformational Leadership

A contemporary model for understanding leadership style considers the leader's purpose and her or his relationships with employees. Burns (1978) suggested that all leaders fit into one of two categories—namely, transactional or transformational leadership—based on this notion.

Transactional leadership can be characterized by the way in which a leader accomplishes an organization's goals and objectives (Seltzer & Bass, 1990). Power and authority are used to gain employees' cooperation, and workers are expected to follow the leader's directives without question. Incentives, often monetary, are linked directly to employee performance and used to motivate increased productivity. However, the effect of these extrinsic rewards seldom is adequate compensation for employees' frustration and resentment, which may ultimately result in their leaving. Transactional leaders often utilize a **punitive** approach, using intimidation and disciplinary actions, such as firing an employee or not granting an anticipated promotion, raise, or day off, to punish poor performance and achieve desired results. Despite their authoritarian ways, transactional leaders work to gain employees' loyalty and cooperation in order to decrease resistance to their approach.

Transformational leaders often assume a creative and visionary approach in their leadership role (Jung, 2001). They appear to be less concerned about achieving specific goals for personal gain. Rather, their primary efforts focus on creating change in an organization and encouraging others to participate in important decisions. Employees, in this style, find that their efforts and contributions are highly valued. The mentoring and inspiration employees receive in the workplace build self-confidence and also contribute to their professional growth. In other words, transformational leaders create a workplace environment that meets employee's individual needs and recognizes their contributions (Bass, 1990). In some situations, the transformational leader may find it necessary to implement change in small steps, or to assign specific tasks to employees who are resistant to change or prefer stronger leadership.

Leaders seldom use one style to the exclusion of the other. Successful leaders often practice a combination of transactional and transformational styles, which gives them maximum flexibility to respond to different circumstances. Both leadership styles offer advantages and disadvantages. For example, the transactional style may be effective for accomplishing things quickly, especially if a project is relatively simple, employees' skills are limited, or there is a short deadline. However, when this style is used exclusively, it can lead to poor employee morale, lack of commitment, and job dissatisfaction. Transformational leaders can be instrumental in energizing employees and moving a program in new directions. However, leaders who practice this style exclusively may become distracted by the process and wind up having limited success.

Connecting Points: Consider a recent situation in which someone else made a decision that affected your behavior.

- Did you feel the decision was appropriate given the circumstances?
- Were your needs and concerns taken into consideration?
- If you could reverse roles, how might your decision differ?

Which Style Is Right?

Successful leaders understand that there is no one best leadership style (Figure 3-7). Leaders who practice a single leadership style find they are not able to respond effectively to organizational needs in many instances. Differences in program structure, goals, objectives, employees, geographic location, and customers, among others factors, require different types of leadership.

Figure 3-7 Effective leaders use multiple leadership styles.

There are several additional criteria leaders can use for deciding on an appropriate leadership style:

■ the nature of the task or problem that is to be addressed.

■ employees' strengths, limitations, values, qualifications, and competency for making particular decisions.

■ how quickly a decision must be made.

■ which players possess the information necessary for making a sound decision.

■ the leader's personality; how comfortable she or he is in turning control or decision-making responsibilities over to others.

Choosing and implementing an effective leadership style requires leaders to carefully assess a situation, modify their behavior, and involve employees whenever it is appropriate. In other words, good decision-making skills enable motivational leaders to optimize their responses to new challenges and changing conditions.

 ## Becoming a Motivational Leader

Motivational leaders distinguish themselves from ordinary leaders by their ability to connect with employees and influence their behavior (Figure 3-8). They inspire performance by acknowledging employees' efforts and contributions, regardless of their significance. For example, a kind word offered to a teacher who has stayed late to meet with an upset parent or a thoughtful note left on an assistant teacher's desk congratulating him on an innovative science activity is a simple act, but it builds an employee's self-confidence and reinforces the likelihood of similar or improved performances in the future.

Motivational leaders willingly invest time and effort in getting to know individual employee's capabilities, limitations, work styles, needs, backgrounds, and comfort levels. They achieve a collaborative spirit by building on individual strengths, encouraging creativity, welcoming employee input, providing constructive feedback, and leading by positive example. Successful leaders maintain open lines of communication and are available for consultation and assistance. They also recognize that employees are in various stages of their professional careers, and so they modify the nature and intensity of their guidance accordingly.

Motivational leaders

- make an effort to see the positive side of situations.
- compliment others frequently.
- encourage others to share their ideas and opinions.
- are patient and good listeners.
- set a good example for others to follow.
- are supportive and encourage others, especially those who may have limited experience with a new task or role.
- believe that a pleasant work environment improves working relationships and productivity.
- look for ways to continually improve their own leadership skills.
- avoid blaming others.
- understand that people make mistakes, and try to use the experience as a learning opportunity.
- respect that others have various needs, concerns, and values, and try to be sensitive to these differences.

Figure 3-8   Characteristics of motivational leaders.

The art of creating enjoyable workplace environments is another trademark of motivational leaders. They continually monitor employee morale and are sensitive to changes in employees' attitudes, appearance, commitment, and work habits. Motivational leaders support and encourage their employees to experiment, create change, and develop their unique potentials. They establish an atmosphere where initiative is appreciated and learning from mistakes is expected. In addition, they recognize that using the force of their position or making excessive demands on employees is unlikely to have positive, long-term outcomes and may contribute instead to their dissatisfaction and eventual departure.

Motivational leaders dedicate themselves to helping employees develop their own personal motivators, thereby reducing their dependency on others for encouragement and reinforcement. Supporting this important transition is a critical step in fostering professional growth among employees. It is accomplished by motivational leaders who empower employees to set personal goals, take advantage of learning opportunities, seek and receive constructive feedback, and accept new challenges and responsibilities.

Leaders must be motivated themselves, before they can successfully motivate others. Thus, it is important for leaders to take time to reflect on their own personal and professional goals and objectives, leadership style, level of commitment, and interpersonal skills. This ongoing process enables leaders not only to evaluate the effectiveness of their decisions and performance but also to consider areas that require improvement. Only then can motivational leaders be effective in their role and serve as an inspiration to employees.

Summary

- Many leaders have no formal training in leadership but end up in leadership positions.
- Effective leadership requires a combination of interests, skills, opportunity, and training.
- Successful leaders have many personal qualities or traits in common.
- Leaders influence almost every functional operation within an organization, from communication to innovation and team building.
- Leadership styles have a direct effect on employee performance and commitment.
- It is important for leaders to be sensitive to cultural differences, personality types, and individual learning styles when mentoring employees.
- The autocratic, consultative, participative, and laissez-faire leadership styles reflect differences in the control and use of power, authority, and decision making.
- Some leaders show greater concern for accomplishing tasks than for building employee relationships.
- A primary objective of transactional leadership is the completion of tasks. Transformational leaders are interested in change and the processes necessary for accomplishing it.
- No single leadership style works effectively in all situations.
- Motivational leaders are able to bring out the best in their employees; they provide support, encouragement, acknowledgement of individual efforts, and inspiration.

Application Activities

1. Identify an employer you consider to be an outstanding leader. Prepare a list of his or her personal leadership qualities and record them on Application Worksheet 3-1.

2. Interview the directors of four early education centers. Find out what they consider to be their most challenging employee motivational needs and what motivators they provide to boost employee morale. Record your results on Application Worksheet 3-2.

3. Read one of these books: *Random Acts of Kindness* by D. Kingma and D. Markova, *Attitudes of Gratitude* by M. J. Ryan, *The 7 Habits of Highly Effective People* by S. R. Covey. Summarize the principles described in the book, and discuss their application for early childhood leaders on Application Worksheet 3-3.

4. Using Application Worksheet 3-4, record your leadership qualities (traits) in one column and your limitations in the other. Select two limitations and develop at least one improvement goal for each. Next, prepare strategies that will help you achieve each of your goals.

Discussion Points

1. Discuss work experiences in which you had a leader who used an autocratic leadership style. Discuss work situations in which a leader used a participative leadership style. What differences did the style have on employee morale and motivation?

2. If a leader had poor communication skills, would it still be possible for her or him to be effective?

3. Debate whether it is necessary for an individual to have formal leadership training as a prerequisite for assuming a leadership position.

Application Worksheet 3-1

Name of the leader you consider to be outstanding _____.

What personal leadership qualities does this person possess?

Why do you admire these qualities?

Which of these personal leadership qualities do you possess?

Which of these qualities would you like to develop? What could you do to begin acquiring these qualities?

Application Worksheet 3-2

After you have recorded the motivational challenges, discuss how typical you think these problems are in early childhood programs. Also, comment on the effectiveness of each motivator identified by the directors.

Director A

Director B

Director C

Director D

Application Worksheet 3-3

Book title: _____

What is the major theme of this book?

Did you find the information helpful or not useful? Explain.

Write a short summary of the main points discussed by the author.

How might you use the information in this book for staff development training?

Application Worksheet 3-4

My leadership qualities: My leadership limitations:

Two limitations I would like to improve:

a.

b.

Strategies to help me achieve my goals:

a.

b.

References

Bass, B. M. (1990, Winter). From transactional to transformational leadership: Learning to share the vision. *Organizational Dynamics,* 19–31.

Blake, R., & Mouton, J. (1964). *The managerial grid.* Houston, TX: Gulf Publishing Co.

Bloom, P. (1997). Navigating the rapids: Directors reflect on their careers and professional development. *Young Children, 52* (7), 32–38.

Burns, J. M. (1978). *Leadership.* New York: Harper & Row.

Gardner, J. (1989). *On leadership.* New York: Free Press.

Horner, M. (2003). Leadership theory: Past, present and future. *Team Performance Management, 3* (4), 270–287.

House, R., & Aditya, R. (1997). The social scientific study of leadership: Quo vadis? *Journal of Management, 23* (3), 409–473.

Jung, D. I. (2001). Transformational and transactional leadership and their effects on creativity in groups. *Creativity Research Journal, 13* (2), 185–195.

Mann, R. (1959). A review of the relationship between personality and performance in small groups. *Psychological Bulletin, 66* (4), 241–270.

Seltzer, J., & Bass, B. (1990). Transformational leadership: Beyond initiation and consideration. *Journal of Mangagement, 16* (4), 693–703.

Stogdill, R. M. (1948). Personal factors associated with leadership. A survey of the literature. *Journal of Psychology, 25,* 35–71.

Vroom, V. (1974). Decision-making and the leadership process. *Journal of Contemporary Business, 3* (4), 47–64.

Yukl, G. A. (1994). *Leadership in organizations* (3rd ed.). Englewood Cliffs, NJ: Prentice Hall (pp. 53–75).

Web Resources

Big Dog's Leadership Guide	*www.nwlink.com*
Changing Minds	*www.changingminds.org/techniques*
FirstGov	*www.firstgov.gov*
Online Women's Business Center	*www.onlinewbc.gov*
Small Business Administration	*www.sba.gov*
U.S. Department of Labor, Bureau of Labor Statistics	*www.bls.gov*

SECTION II
MAKING IT ALL WORK

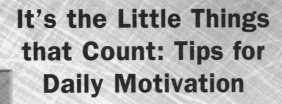

Chapter 4

It's the Little Things that Count: Tips for Daily Motivation

Objectives

After reading this chapter, you will be able to:

- discuss the importance of understanding employees' values and recognition preferences.
- describe effective communication strategies and the ways in which verbal and nonverbal communication differ.
- describe false perceptions employees may have about administrators and the possible impact of their perceptions.
- explain the importance of leader credibility, and discuss how a leader builds credibility with employees.
- discuss how motivational strategies can boost employee morale.

Key Terms

- conflict resolution
- credibility
- invested
- mission
- morale
- retreat
- values

> *"People will forget what you said. People will forget what you did. But people will never forget how you made them feel."*
>
> UNKNOWN

 ## Introduction

At this point, you have a good understanding of motivational theory and the challenges that face early childhood leaders and teaching staff who work in early childhood settings. The remaining chapters of this book are designed to stimulate your imagination and to expand your repertoire of motivational skills. Now, it is time to have some fun!

The Importance of Getting to Know Your Employees

The motivational leader must take steps to learn much more about an individual than simply his or her qualifications for a given job. We must learn to ask questions, listen, and identify a person's talents, limitations, personal values, and professional goals. An employee's career stage is also important to consider so that motivators are developmentally appropriate. The motivational leader must also care about and respect employees who choose to resist their efforts.

Simple But Effective Ways to Say "You're Important"

The remainder of this chapter includes descriptions of everyday strategies that can be implemented easily in a variety of settings. Some are designed to help you to get to know your employees and their personal **values,** while others will help you learn about their individual preferences for recognition and rewards. Collectively, these strategies will help you to practice a positive motivational style of leadership.

■ *"Getting to know you" meetings*—Schedule brief meetings with each employee to discuss anything she or he would like to share with you—anything from workplace issues, suggestions for improvement, recent experiences or accomplishments, family photographs, a vacation, to information about hobbies or children (Figure 4-1). Posting a sign-up sheet lets employees know when you are available and assures that interruptions will be minimal. Provide simple refreshments, such as fresh fruit, popcorn, beverages, or cookies to create a relaxed, **retreat**-like atmosphere.

■ *Strengths and work preference survey*—Develop a survey form and ask employees to identify their perceived strengths and indicate their interests in serving on committees or assisting with special projects.

■ *Team assessment*—Conduct a personality assessment as a team activity. Utilize one of the many evaluation tools available online, or published in books, that address individual qualities, such as personality, communication styles, **conflict resolution** skills, and work styles. Discuss the strengths and weaknesses of a given style as a team; try to analyze the style's effect on working

Figure 4-1   Schedule "getting to know you" meetings with individual employees.

relationships. Discuss how the information can be used to build team solidarity and to help people with different styles understand each other. Your local child care resource and referral agency or county research and extension office may be able to assist with professional training. True Colors® is widely used in professional circles, and its focus is on team development. Extend this activity by creating a bulletin board in an employee area of the center, where each person's style is posted along with the style definitions and team-building information. Be sure to let participants know in advance that this information will be posted and that sharing this information is a critical part of the team-building activity. Emphasize that there are no right or wrong answers and that the diversity of the group is what makes the team stronger. Allowing each person to learn about the team members' individual communication styles, work styles, and conflict resolution/problem-solving styles will bring about a greater understanding of individual strengths and overall team dynamics. If implemented correctly, this activity will not label an individual but will emphasize strengths and style preferences with room for personal growth and change. Sharing this information will create a stronger team by building on these strengths and preferences.

■ *Recognition and rewards survey*—Survey employees to find out what reward is most meaningful to them for a "job well done." It is important to learn whether a person prefers public or private recognition as well as what kinds of recognition are meaningful. One employee may take great pride in public recognition, while another may be embarrassed. Leaders may also use food, particularly candy or bakery items, to celebrate accomplishments or as small gestures of appreciation. However, food may not be rewarding to someone with dietary restrictions; a sincere note of appreciation may have the most meaningful impact in these instances.

■ *Employee committees*—Create opportunities for employees to work together, and as individuals, on projects that reinforce a program's goals and **mission** (Figure 4-2). When employees feel a sense of ownership in the overall program, they become **invested** and begin to feel that they have a crucial role in a program's success. Employees can also be involved in developing recognition programs and social events. Be sure each committee develops guidelines and goals, so they do not become an unproductive outlet for employee complaints.

Figure 4-2 Employee committees promote a sense of ownership.

- *"A cookie for your thoughts" meeting*—In the spirit of "a penny for your thoughts," schedule a time each month when you are available for an informal meeting with employees. Let them create the agenda, ask questions, discuss employee issues, or simply spend quality time with administration. These meetings could have a come-and-go format and be scheduled during naptime so teachers can take turns leaving the classroom (always be sure to maintain the required teacher/child ratios). Refreshments also encourage people to stop in and help create a more relaxed atmosphere. Making time available to listen to employees lets them know that you value their ideas and concerns.

- *Room rounds*—Get to know employees by getting out of the front office and into the classrooms. Motivational leaders understand that visibility and communication with employees are key to healthy **morale.** Employees want their leader to understand and appreciate what they deal with on a daily basis and to experience their work environment. Set an alarm, use a timer, or schedule a pop-up reminder in a computer calendar/ scheduling program as a prompt to take a break and develop relationships with people.

- *Team development*—Make use of team-building activities as a fun way for employees to get to know each other and learn to work together better. You can create a series of "challenge" activities that require people to work together to accomplish a group task. Groups can be preselected; this approach can move people out of their comfort zones and require employees who may have little daily interaction to work together. A simple way to preselect is to color-code name tags or place settings, and then ask each of the colors to form a group.

Here are some examples of mixers and "getting to know you" activities.

- *Staff scavenger hunt*—Find a person who fits a prewritten statement (e.g., "has more than three children, lives within 3 miles of the center, and has been to the top of the Statue of Liberty"). (See Appendix B.)

- *Two truths and a lie*—Have each person write two truths and one lie about him- or herself. Then others try to guess which is the lie.

- *Take as much as you like*—Pass a bowl of multicolored candy around, and then instruct the group to tell something about themselves for each red piece of candy they have.

Many Web sites that describe small- and large-group activities are available on the Internet. Conduct a search using the keywords "team building," "team-building activities," and "team-building games."

Nonmonetary Strategies to Encourage Performance and Commitment

Motivational leaders create environments in which employees find their work interesting, challenging, purposeful, and appreciated (Figure 4-3). They discuss program goals and objectives clearly, so employees understand what they are collectively and individually expected to achieve. Motivational leaders encourage employee input and provide opportunities for employees to express their ideas and suggestions for position and program improvement. They understand that when employees have a sense of ownership in decisions affecting a program's success, they are more likely to remain committed to the organization. Imagine, for example, an organization whose entire staff works on a voluntary basis, and consider what conditions would make them want to return to work again and again.

In 1983, the Public Agenda Foundation conducted a survey to determine the factors employees considered most rewarding in their work (Yankelovich, 1983). Although this study is now more than 20 years old, the results still have application today. The items are ordered beginning with most rewarding.

1. Work with people who treat them with respect.
2. Do interesting work.
3. Receive recognition for doing a good job.
4. Have a chance to develop new skills.
5. Work for people who listen to you if you have ideas about how to do things better.
6. Have chances to think for themselves, rather than just carry out instructions.
7. See the results of their work.
8. Work for efficient managers.
9. Have a job that is not too easy.
10. Be well informed about what is going on.
11. Have job security.
12. Receive high pay.
13. Receive good benefits.

Clearly, something beyond money or benefits must serve as a motivator if you want an emotional investment from your employees and to have them remain with a program.

Source: D. Yankelovich. (1983). *Putting the work ethic to work.* New York: Public Agenda Foundation.

Figure 4-3 Employee motivational preferences.

Effective leaders utilize multiple strategies to motivate employee performance. They must establish a relationship of mutual trust and **credibility** with employees in order to gain their respect and cooperation. As employees gain confidence in their leader, their own sense of self-confidence and self-esteem often improves. An effective strategy commonly used by successful leaders involves open and frequent communication with employees (Figure 4-4). When motivation becomes a daily practice, leaders and peers begin to focus less time and effort on an individual's limitations and mistakes. Instead, these experiences become positive learning opportunities that ultimately enhance an employee's performance and professional development.

Figure 4-4   Frequent communication with employees builds trust and confidence.

The Director's Showcase

What motivational strategies have you found effective in boosting staff morale?

"Listening, listening, listening to staff with sincerity and understanding! Saying 'thank you' on a regular basis lets staff know how much you appreciate their efforts. I have also found that holding poor performers accountable for less than acceptable performance or attitude has had a positive effect on all staff members. It sends the message to everyone that we are committed to high standards."

Patricia Maddox, Director
Dealey Child Care Center
Presbyterian Hospital of Dallas, TX

Strategies for Effective Communication

As they say in real estate, "It's all about location, location, location." Motivational leaders understand that when they manage a group of people, it's all about communication, communication, communication. Employees want to know what is happening in the organization. They want to be informed, to understand the "big picture," and to have a voice. A breakdown in communication quickly breeds frustration and negativity. We suggest some tools to enhance effective communication.

- *Daily Report*—The Daily Report is distributed each morning and includes information such as: the center mission statement; an inspirational quote; special event announcements; employee birthdays; appreciation "kudos" for employees coming in early, staying late, making extra efforts, and so on; "FYI," including organizational updates, reminders, policy information, and information that may affect the day; the weather forecast for the day, including any health alerts that may restrict outdoor play; and a staffing report, including a list of any substitutes or agency staff, classrooms in which they are working, and scheduled and unscheduled staff absences for the day. (This also helps raise awareness of frequent absentees and heightens employee accountability.)

- *Monday Morning News*—This is a weekly version of the Daily Report or may be an additional communication to brighten Monday mornings with inspirational information and humor.

- *Suggestion Box*—An employee suggestion box allows people to ask questions they may not want to ask in person. You may wish to set guidelines, such as a statement that any complaints must include suggestions for improvement. Comments are then collected monthly (or more frequently if manageable), and a written response to each comment is distributed to all staff. You may also want to create a catchy title such as "Communication Station" or "Ask (Director Name)." While some comments may seem somewhat negative, the procedure allows frustrations to surface, and the director can address them with policy, procedure, center goals, and action plan information. This is an opportunity to redirect negative frustrations toward positive solutions. For example, questions that address employee performance issues can be responded to with a specific policy, an explanation of the corrective action plan process, and a reminder that all performance issues are addressed in a confidential manner.

- *Communication Log*—Placing a communication notebook at the front desk and in each classroom facilitates communication between employees who are working on different shifts.

- *Bathroom Bulletin*—As silly as this may sound, posting information on the back of the bathroom door is an effective way to get people's attention.

■ *Substitute Staff Notebook*—You may create an information note-book for each classroom covering important information that a substitute teacher would need to know. The notebook should include administrative contact information and where the sub-stitute can locate supplies, first aid equipment, and child record information.

■ *Team Meetings*—It is important to bring all employees together to discuss team issues in order to create opportunities for effective communication, collaboration, professional develop-ment, team building, and goal setting. Each meeting should have an agenda and a time frame, and you should follow them (Figure 4-5). By keeping the meeting on track and within its time frame, you are demonstrating respect for your employees' time and personal lives. You may want to create a "parking lot" for nonagenda issues that come up and cannot be addressed during that meeting. The "parking lot" is a catchy title for a way to document issues that cannot be addressed, so that you acknowledge the issues and remember to discuss them at a future meeting. A flip chart or dry erase board may be used to record parking lot items, which are then added to your next meeting's agenda or delegated to smaller committees to address and to report their recommendations back to the group. Also,

Figure 4-5 Team meetings should have an agenda and a set time frame.

someone should be assigned to take minutes and distribute them to all employees following the meeting.

■ *Round Table Discussion*—Time should be set aside at each team meeting for "round table," which gives each person an opportunity to raise any suggestions, comments, or concerns.

Connecting Points: Take a moment to think about someone in a position of authority or influence whom you believed to be credible and trustworthy.

■ What did this person do to earn your confidence and trust?

■ What leadership qualities did he or she demonstrate?

■ Compare this person with someone who lost credibility as a leader. Explain how the two were different.

■ When a leader loses credibility and trust with employees, how difficult is it to regain their trust? Explain.

■ What is the most important leadership quality to build and maintain credibility with employees?

Strategies for Building Trust and Credibility

"We want to believe in our leaders. We want to have faith and confidence in them as people. We want to believe that their word can be trusted, that they have the knowledge and skill to lead, and that they are personally excited and enthusiastic about the direction in which we are headed. Credibility is the foundation of leadership" (Kouzes & Posner, 1993).

Being a trustworthy leader and developing a climate of trust among employees will have a positive impact on morale. Consistency and effective communication help to build trust; when your actions match your words, you also gain credibility (Figure 4-6). Be aware of your communication style as well as the verbal and non-verbal messages you may be sending. Actions really do speak louder than words. Studies show that when we are speaking, the listener interprets most of the message through our nonverbal means of communication. Noted psychologist Albert Mehrabian (1981) has shown that 55 percent of a message is interpreted through body language, 38 percent through tone of voice, and only 7 percent through our actual words. With this in mind, it is essential to make sure that your

Trust is fundamental to the success of an organization. Leaders should follow these guidelines to build trust with their employees.

- *Be fair:* Trustworthy leaders develop clear standards, explain the decision-making process, make unbiased decisions, and involve employees in decisions whenever possible.

- *Be consistent:* Trustworthy leaders are stable, reliable, dependable, and consistent; employees learn they can depend on their decisions.

- *Keep promises:* Leaders make only those promises that they are able and willing to keep; they follow through on responsibilities and projects.

- *Act with integrity:* They practice honesty and demonstrate trustworthiness.

- *Make a decision and stick with it:* Trustworthy leaders are competent and communicate with confidence. They are willing to take a stand, make mistakes, take ownership of mistakes, and learn from them.

- *Listen:* They listen carefully to what employees have to say.

- *Maintain the highest level of confidentiality:* They avoid gossip and favoritism.

- *Walk their talk:* Trustworthy leaders reinforce words with action, model desired behavior, and don't ask others to do something they aren't willing to do.

- *Be loyal:* They let their employees know they can be counted on for respect and support in difficult times.

- *Hold everyone accountable to the same rules:* Trustworthy leaders develop clear guidelines and boundaries, hold everyone accountable to the same standards, and enforce them consistently. Inconsistent treatment can lead to a perception of favoritism.

- *Trust others:* They create an atmosphere of trust by respecting others' decisions; they allow employees to make mistakes and learn from them without fear of repercussion.

Figure 4-6 How to build trust.

body language and tone are consistent with the message you want to communicate (Figure 4-7).

Also, look at environmental factors that may be sending the wrong message. Many offices are furnished with modular desks and shelving units placed against a wall. If this requires you to sit with your back to the door, you may unintentionally be sending a message that you are unapproachable (Figure 4-8). If rearranging furniture is not an option, try using a mirror so that you can see when people approach; turn to greet them or post a friendly sign: "Welcome, please let me know you are here."

> *Body language conveys messages that are just as powerful as spoken words. When communicating with employees, remember these tips.*
>
> ▨ Always speak in a calm, professional manner. Remain calm and professional no matter what the employee may be saying or doing.
>
> ▨ Approach confrontations in a professional manner; the hotter the confrontation gets, the cooler (calmer) you should become.
>
> ▨ Maintain direct eye contact. Be sure to look the employee in the eye, but avoid staring in a confrontational manner.
>
> ▨ Sit in a relaxed, "open" body position. Remember that folding your arms across your chest can appear defensive.
>
> ▨ Position yourself leaning toward the employee. This posture communicates that you are interested and the employee has your full attention.

Figure 4-7 Basic body language concepts.

Finally, consider your work routine and habits. Employees often have very unrealistic perceptions of leaders' intentions or how they spend their time as a result of nonverbal factors. Here are some real life examples.

▨ Program Coordinator Janie spends most of the day in her office, frequently with the door closed. When employees see her in the office, she is usually either on the phone or drinking coffee. She always has a coffee mug in her hand as she walks through the classrooms. Employees frequently comment that the only things Janie does all day are drink coffee and talk on the phone.

▨ Director Tom and his administrative team spend a lot of time working at their office computers. Comments in the suggestion box express frustration that supervisors are spending their time surfing the Internet at leisure, e-mailing friends, and shopping online.

▨ Supervisor Marie is very demonstrative in her communication style. She frequently uses hand gestures as she speaks, and her tone of voice becomes loud and emotional when she deals with stressful situations. Employees frequently complain that they feel they have been verbally attacked, and state that Marie shakes her finger at them in a scolding manner. Marie does not realize that she is perceived as an aggressive person. Her perception is that she is just very passionate about her work and committed to doing things right.

Figure 4-8 Facing the office door conveys a message that you are approachable.

Perception is powerful. These kinds of negative perceptions can be counteracted by being visible, giving employees your full attention, taking the time to get to know employees, and being fully aware of your own communication style and how it is perceived by others.

Connecting Points: Think about a time when you had a negative perception of someone in a leadership role.

- What nonverbal factors influenced your perception?
- How could those nonverbal factors have been changed? Would this have resulted in a change in your perception of the event?
- How can misunderstandings occur based on nonverbal factors?

Strategies for Nurturing Positive Thoughts

Positive thinking leads to positive action. For many people, it is easier to focus on the negative aspects of the day and the things that have gone wrong. Some people seem to be happy only when they are complaining about something or someone. Consider using the following strategies as a means to help employees focus on the things that are going well: How can negative energy be turned into positive thoughts and action?

- *Praise cards*—Create preprinted notes of appreciation. Place them in public areas so they are easily available to employees and parents. You may want to create a space where the notes are posted for a period of time. Copies may be included in an employee's performance file, so that they can be considered during an annual performance evaluation.

- *Caught in the act of caring*—Use fish-shaped notes to recognize people who have provided service excellence through caring and kindness. Create a bulletin board with a large net, into which people can place the notes or deliver notes attached to a clothespin fishing pole.

- *Gratitude journals*—Encourage positive thinking by giving a notebook to each employee; ask people to use them for happy thoughts, such as personal accomplishments, things they are thankful for, and positive moments of the day. You may want to include a "special" pen (colored, sparkle, etc.). Extend this idea by creating a reward system for those who use their journals.

- *Inspirational reading*—Post inspirational quotes and posters throughout the center. Place early childhood books, magazines, and other inspirational and humorous reading materials in the break room. To encourage reading, tape a coupon to a page in the book or magazine that can be exchanged for a reward. For example, "Thank you for taking the time to keep current with early childhood issues and trends! Bring this coupon to the front office to exchange for a free item of your choice from the vending machines."

- *"Graffiti" board*—Hang a dry erase board or poster-sized paper with a starter phrase, and ask employees to share their thoughts (Figure 4-9). Sample starter phrases:
  - "I enjoy working here because . . ."
  - "My favorite childhood memory is . . ."
  - "The funniest thing a child ever said to me was . . ."

- *"Pass it on"*—During a team meeting, pass around individual sheets of stationery that have a single employee's name written at the top. As the paper goes around the table, all team

Figure 4-9   Employees can share their thoughts on a graffiti board.

members write something they appreciate about that person. When the paper returns to the owner, it is full of positive thoughts and encouragement.

- *Group sharing*—Make time at each team meeting to share positive thoughts, joys, and meaningful events from the day.
- *"Getting to know you" notebook*—Create a notebook that has information about each employee's hobbies, leisure-time activities, favorite things (foods, beverages, collectibles), family information, and pets, and keep them in the break room for staff members to read.
- *"Pat on the back"*—Cut out paper hands and use them to write your notes of appreciation, and give them to employees as a "pat on the back." Or, trace two hands, joined at the base of the palms (where the paper will be folded), and give this note of appreciation as a "round of applause." When the recipient opens and closes the note, it will appear to be clapping.

Strategies to Practice Random Acts of Kindness

Many early childhood programs celebrate Teacher Appreciation Week, which is a wonderful opportunity to celebrate our profession and to show appreciation for each other and our dedication to children. Why limit that to one week per year? The following activities are simple and inexpensive ways to practice random acts of kindness and celebrate each other throughout the year.

Everyday Stress Busters

- Place fresh flowers in the break room for a cheery surprise.
- Order pizza on "fish stick" day!
- Order, or make your own, healthy fruit smoothies to celebrate a team accomplishment.
- Show your appreciation with "The Gift of Time" coupons, which can be a legitimate late-arrival pass, a leave-early pass, or an award of extra help in the classroom (Figure 4-10).
- Show your appreciation with a "Mess Pass," a coupon that can be exchanged for diaper duty or cleaning up a classroom mess.

Figure 4-10 Leader-made coupons can be used to show employees your appreciation.

- *"Have a 'coke' and a smile"*—Cans of soda or juice can be purchased in bulk at a very low cost (be sure to discover employees' favorite brands and flavors). Keep a supply of these beverages available, and on stressful days, send out the message, "Have a 'coke' and a smile. . . . I'll provide the 'coke' if you provide the smile." It is amazing how an inexpensive can of soda or juice will brighten someone's day.

- *"Cheers to You" basket*—Watch for sales, and purchase inexpensive items (e.g., lotions, candles, candy, bubbles, notepads). Make a basket of them to let someone who is experiencing a stressful day know that you care.

- Potluck luncheons are a fun way to spend social time together. Also, try an ice cream social; provide a smorgasbord of sundae toppings. An employee luncheon prepared by the administration is a wonderful way to show your appreciation. Employees will enjoy being "served" by their administrators, and it is also a fun way for administrators to bond with one another.

- Arrange for a massage therapist to provide chair massages in a quiet area of the center. Chair massages typically cost $1 per minute: staff can sign up and pay for their own massages. You can also purchase inexpensive massage chair cushions for the break room.

- Celebrate employee wellness! Have a party after a lengthy period of time during which no employees were out due to illness. Create incentive programs that reward attendance, such as a bonus for best attendance in a six-month period or a holiday leave priority based on past attendance. Develop a wellness committee that plans activities, such as a break-time walking group or after-hours aerobics.

- Create an employee "Welcome Wagon" committee to greet and welcome newly hired employees. On a new employee's first day, greet her or him with posters in the hallway, a friendly note or small gift, an invitation to share a lunch break, and a welcoming peer to contact with any questions.

- Secret pals are fun any time of the year. Keep it simple with notes of appreciation or inexpensive items. Birthday buddies will make sure someone is recognized and feels special on his or her birthday. Simply draw names at the beginning of the year and include an information sheet that describes the likes and dislikes of each participant.

- Encourage employees to organize motivation and appreciation activities. Find out who the "party planners" are on your team, and build on those strengths by empowering them to lead a morale committee.

Everyday Appreciation The following sample list of fun phrases can be attached to various items or candy. Use computer-printed labels to make quick and easy phrases to attach. Once you are in this mind-set, it is simple to create clever phrases and bring a smile to someone's day. Keep some of these items on hand, so that you can immediately extend a small gesture of appreciation when there is an occasion. The possibilities are endless!

- Jar of nuts—"We're nuts about you!"
- Kudos bar—"KUDOS to you!"
- Lifesavers—"You're a real life saver!"
- Candle—"A candle to light when you are feeling burned out."
- Markers—"Mark my words, you are outstanding!"
- Highlighter—"Thanks, that was the highlight of my day!"
- Eraser—"Everyone makes mistakes. I know that you will learn something positive from this one."
- Carefree gum—"Have a carefree day!"
- Payday bar—"Hurray! It's pay day!"
- Glue stick—"Thanks for sticking together to support each other!"
- Popcorn—"I may be CORNY, but our center POPS with excitement, enthusiasm, and excellence because you are here!"
- Air freshener—"You're a breath of fresh air."
- Photo frame—"Thanks for always being in a positive frame of mind."
- Pair of "fun" design socks—"Thanks for putting your best foot forward."
- Stickers—"Stick with it; you will do great!"
- Gummy bears—"We are beary glad you're here!"
- Gummy frogs—"You are toad-ally awesome!"
- Baby Ruth bar—"You really hit a home run on that project!"
- Whoppers—"We have a whopper of a team!"

- Puzzle pieces glued to picture frame—"Without you, our team is not complete."
- Chalk—"Chalk it up to a job well done."
- Flower—"If teachers were flowers, we'd pick you."
- Glitter glue—"Thanks for the extra sparkle!"
- Lightbulb—"You light up our lives!" (written in permanent marker)
- Multicolored candy—"Teacher Pep Pills: Green for energy; Orange for humor; Yellow for cheerfulness; Black for moodiness; Blue for light stress; Purple for heavy stress; RED ONLY FOR EMERGENCIES!"

Survival Kits   Survival kits are designed around a common theme and include a variety of related items. These kits can be created for any occasion with a little creativity. A list of items that can be included in each of the following kits is provided in Appendix A.

- Teacher Survival Kit
- Team Builders Survival Kit
- Wellness Survival Kit
- Stress Busters Survival Kit
- New Teacher Survival Kit

Summary

- Employees have different motivational needs based on their individual values, personalities, and goals.
- Motivational leaders must learn about and respect an individual's recognition preferences, and understand that what motivates one employee may not be effective for another person.
- It is important for leaders to be visible and available to their employees.
- Motivational leaders can develop empathy with the issues and frustrations employees experience on a daily basis by spending time in their classrooms and other workplace areas.

- Motivational leaders seek employees' input and participation in achieving program goals and objectives.
- Effective leaders utilize multiple strategies to motivate employee performance.
- Motivational leaders set aside time to develop relationships with employees and to build mutual trust and respect.
- Effective communication is essential for the success of the program.
- Employees want and expect to be informed, to understand the big picture, and to have a voice.
- Nonverbal messages may undermine a leader's credibility by creating false, negative perceptions.
- Leaders cannot force employees to do great things, but they can create an environment where employees are motivated to do great things.

Application Activities

1. Use your creativity, and add at least five items to the list of "Everyday Appreciation" suggestions provided in this chapter. Record your items on Application Worksheet 4-1.

2. Use Application Worksheet 4-2 to develop a "Find someone who" questionnaire that will help you learn more about your colleagues, employees, or team members. Use your questionnaire before a staff meeting or orientation session to encourage participant interaction.

3. Conduct an online search using the keywords "team building," "team-building activities," and "team-building games." Use Application Worksheet 4-3 to compile a list of at least eight sites that you found informative and would recommend to others. Prepare a brief description of the resources you found at each site.

4. Have someone videotape you while you are working in the classroom, conducting a meeting, or conversing with a parent or employee. View the tape, and evaluate your body language. What positive or negative messages might you be sending to others? Record your observations on Application Worksheet 4-4, and develop a goal to address any negative messages.

Application Worksheet 4-1

My "Everyday Appreciation" ideas

1.

2.

3.

4.

5.

Refer back to the information presented in Chapter 2. What motivational needs does each of these motivators fulfill for employees?

Application Worksheet 4-2

Continue to add statements to the list below. When you are finished, use your questionnaire at the next staff meeting, and then evaluate how successful it was in eliciting new information about your colleagues.

"Find Someone Who" Questionnaire

1. Somebody who enjoys cooking is _____.

2. Someone who walks or runs at least one mile each day is _____.

3. _____ has attended a NAEYC annual conference.

4. Someone who knows what a solstice is _____.

5.

6.

7.

8.

9.

10.

11.

12.

Application Worksheet 4-3

Web sites I found most informative and useful

1.

2.

3.

4.

5.

6.

7.

8.

Application Worksheet 4-4

After viewing the videotape of yourself in action, what behaviors and actions did you identify?

Body language that conveyed a positive message

Body language that could send a negative message

List goals to improve your negative actions.

Discussion Points

1. What is credibility? Why is it important for leaders to establish credibility in the workplace?
2. How do employee perceptions influence behavior?
3. What role does communication play in the workplace? What are some ways motivational leaders can maintain effective communication with employees?
4. How does body language influence communication?

References

Kouzes, J., & Posner, B. (1993). *Credibility: How leaders gain and lose it, why people demand it.* San Francisco, CA: Jossey-Bass.

Mehrabian, A. (1981). *Silent messages: Implicit communication of emotions and attitudes.* Belmont, CA: Wadsworth.

Yankelovich, D. (1983). *Putting the work ethic to work.* New York: Public Agenda Foundation.

Web Resources

True Colors	*www.truecolors.org*
Nelson Motivation Inc.	*www.nelson-motivation.com*
Baudville	*www.baudville.com*
Successories	*www.successories.com*
The Random Acts of Kindness Foundation	*www.actsofkindness.org*
National Association for Employee Recognition	*www.recognition.org*
Administrators.net	*www.administrators.net*

Chapter 5

Organizational Incentives

Objectives

After reading this chapter, you will be able to:

- discuss the importance of intrinsic rewards.
- understand and demonstrate effective praise and feedback.
- discuss the effectiveness of these reward strategies: job design, mentoring, empowerment, and professional development.
- explain the key elements of job design: expansion, enrichment, and exchange.

Key Terms

- accountable
- collaborative
- cross-training
- empowerment
- feedback

- incentives
- in-service
- mentoring
- productivity

> *"People often say that motivation doesn't last. Well, neither does bathing—that's why we recommend it daily."*
>
> ZIG ZIGLAR

 ## Introduction

Why is it that some people look forward to going to work and will do whatever it takes to get a job done, while others dread going to work and find it difficult to meet the minimum performance expectations? In this chapter, we will discuss several strategies that are designed to reward employees and to improve their morale. We will also provide helpful guidelines for giving effective praise and feedback to employees. In addition, we will present ideas for motivating employees through job restructuring and professional development opportunities.

 ## A Closer Look at Reward Systems

Reward systems that are meaningful and valued by an employee have a positive impact on behavior. Designing a reward system that attracts and helps retain qualified individuals—as well as motivates desired performance—is an ongoing challenge in many early childhood programs. Successful motivational systems match the reward to the person and achievement, and they are timely and specific (Figure 5-1). Ideally, they also provide a combination of extrinsic and intrinsic incentives for optimizing employee performance and commitment.

Intrinsic rewards provide the greatest impact and can have a lifelong effect. They foster employees' feelings of **empowerment** to make decisions and take risks, self-esteem and confidence, and daily success. They provide an internal feeling of accomplishment, which adds an incentive to keep working toward a goal. Leaders who utilize intrinsic rewards work toward job design and enhanced working conditions in such a way that people feel rewarded and motivated by the work itself (Lieberman, 1995). When employees are motivated intrinsically, there is little need for leadership to constantly monitor, measure, and manage employees' behavior.

Figure 5-1 Successful motivational systems match the reward to the person and achievement.

In contrast, extrinsic rewards do not lead to the same feelings of fulfillment and long-term commitment. They may have immediate and cumulative impacts on employee motivation, but these are most often transient effects that must be continually reinforced. Monetary **incentives,** such as increased wages, bonuses, or additional benefits packages, are examples of extrinsic rewards commonly used to recognize employee performance; however, financial resources for such incentives are limited in many early childhood programs. Although improved compensation remains a pressing issue in the field, it should not be viewed as the only strategy available for motivating employee performance.

Motivational leaders who take a creative approach can find numerous opportunities in the workplace to reinforce employees' efforts. For example, leaders should consider elements of the job itself that employees find rewarding. Praise, performance evaluations, and frequent feedback can be powerful motivators. Job design—expansion, enrichment, and exchange—offers motivational leaders another effective strategy for encouraging and rewarding exceptional performance. Providing opportunities for professional development, such as professional journals for employees to read, tuition assistance, and time off to attend **in-service** training, conveys a sense of genuine caring and interest in meeting employees' personal and professional needs. In addition, these and similar approaches can have a renewing and energizing effect on employees' performance.

In the remainder of this chapter, we will explore several alternative types of reward systems and discuss their implementation in early education settings.

Praise

Studies and employee satisfaction surveys have shown that, first and foremost, employees prefer verbal forms of recognition and **feedback** from their supervisors, followed by recognition and feedback in written form. Other types of recognition and rewards, such as monetary bonuses, are considered less desirable. Employees want their leaders to be involved, observing them in their work, providing daily feedback, and offering appreciation for their efforts. Leaders who are viewed as being accessible, responsive to employees' needs, **collaborative,** and respectful are able to build long-lasting, positive relationships with employees.

When giving praise, the leader is not only reinforcing the observed behaviors but also encouraging future positive behaviors, such as initiative, risk taking, openness to change, and professional growth. To be effective, praise and feedback must have these characteristics.

- *Be timely:* To be most effective, praise should come as soon as possible after the achievement or desired behavior has occurred. Praise that is delayed for days will lose its significance.

- *Be sincere:* Praise should always be genuine and given when a supervisor is truly appreciative of an accomplishment or behavior (Figure 5-2). Otherwise, it may be perceived as a form of manipulation, something offered only when leadership stands to benefit—for example, providing praise only when employees come to work early or stay late.

- *Be specific:* Just as with the children, praise for employees should be descriptive and specific. Generalities such as "good job" sound hollow. An employee wants to know exactly what

Figure 5-2 Praise should be sincere and timely.

she or he did that was of value; for example, "I watched your circle time activity this morning, and I could tell that you spent a lot of time planning and preparing for your lesson. The children were very engaged and enjoyed it. Thank you."

- *Be personal:* Delivering praise to employees in person makes it more meaningful and sincere. This effort also sends an important message to employees; it lets them know they are important enough for you to set aside everything else and focus your time and attention on them.

Simple Ways to Praise

- Say thank you, and be specific!
- Catch people in the act of doing something positive, and tell them what you liked and why.
- Write a thank you note.
- Write a personal note telling someone why you value him or her as an employee.
- Write a note of appreciation, and send it to the employee's home.
- Include a note of appreciation with the payroll check.

- Include a "staff highlights" section in your monthly newsletter, recognizing a different employee each month for his or her special efforts or contributions.

- Encourage parents and peer employees to write notes of appreciation by making note cards or note pads available at the front desk.

- Create an employee recognition bulletin board.

- Include "kudos" as an agenda item for team meetings.

- Take pictures of employees "in action," and post the pictures with captions that describe their efforts and dedication.

- Request a note of thanks from a higher-level supervisor to recognize an employee's accomplishment.

- When program tours are given, introduce employees by name and mention why they are assets to the team.

Feedback

Providing employees with feedback is a fundamental part of a leader's role. Effective feedback builds trust, establishes open communication, motivates employees, rewards good performance, and improves performance. It should be delivered in formal and informal ways throughout the year (see Appendix C). Feedback provided only in an annual review is insufficient and ineffective for promoting professional growth. Employees generally want to know how they are performing, and whether or not they are meeting expectations and performance goals. Do not let employees assume that they know how they are doing or that "no news is good news."

Motivational leaders understand the value of constructive feedback and take time in their days to give useful feedback to employees. Through this process, they send the message, "I care about you, notice you, and value you." Ongoing positive and negative feedback builds trust in leadership and helps the employee become more **accountable.** When giving feedback, be sure to keep the following guidelines in mind:

- Focus on the behavior, not the person or attitude. Explain how behaviors have an impact on the employee's ability to meet expectations.

- Always be specific about the behavior you appreciated or hope to correct.

Figure 5-3   Use "I" messages to avoid putting an employee on the defensive.

- Take time to listen; find out what the employee's perceptions are before you attempt to address her or him.
- Describe what you want, not what you don't want.
- Use "I" messages, such as "I observed" or "I understand," rather than stating, "You need to . . .," which typically puts the receiver on the defensive (Figure 5-3).
- Acknowledge feelings; you may not agree with an employee's explanation or reason, but attempting to understand and acknowledge the employee's feelings will promote better collaboration.
- Seek solutions together; collaborate so that the employee buys in. Encourage the employee to think of solutions to problems.
- Develop a plan for improvement. Determine the next steps to reach an improvement goal. Make sure that the employee understands what she or he needs to do in order to be successful.
- Ask questions to make sure that the employee has a clear understanding of the issues that prompted your conversation.
- Summarize the discussion. Restate the issue, the solutions that were discussed, and the next course of action. Be sure to offer your support and assistance.

- Follow up. Observe performance and improvement. Catch the employee doing things right, and offer praise to reinforce the behavior.
- Reevaluate and discuss progress, and make changes as necessary.
- Lead by example. Make sure that there are no double standards: leaders follow the same rules and expectations that are set for employees.

Providing feedback throughout the year will help to ensure that employees are making progress toward professional goals and that there are no surprises at the time of their annual performance review. Document all discussions involving feedback so that you can track the employee's progress or continue to identify performance problems. Be sure to document praise as well as corrective discussions, and keep copies of notes received from parents or other staff members praising an employee's performance. This information will come in handy when you work on formal reviews.

However, keep in mind that the feedback path should not be in only one direction: from leaders to employees. It is also important for the leader to solicit feedback from employees to ensure that she or he is meeting employee expectations. This step will yield valuable information that a leader can use to increase effectiveness, improve communication, and create a workplace environment that employees find motivating.

Job Design

Job design is the process by which leaders determine individual job tasks and authority. The leader's goal is to design jobs that will be motivational for employees based on each employee's individual needs, aspects of the job itself, and the work environment. Making changes to job design is intended to provide more intrinsic rewards that are derived from the work itself (Figure 5-4). Job design attempts to identify the most important needs of the employee and the organization, and to remove workplace obstacles that hinder the satisfaction of those needs.

Carefully designed jobs maximize employee motivation and improve **productivity,** attendance, morale, teamwork, and program effectiveness (Luce, 1998). Job demands that are matched to an employee's abilities and interests also boost job satisfaction.

Figure 5-4   Making changes in an employee's job responsibilities can be highly motivating.

Sometimes simple changes in an employee's job can make a big difference in morale.

Three different approaches can be used in designing jobs: job expansion, job enrichment, and job exchange. Each involves a slightly different modification of an employee's current responsibilities.

Job Expansion.   Job expansion is a process in which a job is made larger in scope by incorporating new tasks. The goal is to increase employee motivation by assigning additional, varied, or novel tasks. We present three examples of job expansion in an early childhood program:

- Modifying the organizational structure to involve more than an administrative director and assistant director. "Program Coordinators" or "Unit Supervisors" for each area of the center can act as direct supervisors for those areas (e.g., Office Coordinator, Curriculum Coordinator, Infant Supervisor, Toddler Supervisor). Each coordinator is responsible for hiring, training, supervising, observing, and conducting performance evaluations for employees in the given area. In addition, coordinators may be responsible for tasks that are part of the overall center operation (e.g., preparing classroom supply budgets, writing a program newsletter, maintaining records). This arrangement encourages professional growth and provides opportunities for promotion.

■ Developing opportunities for employees to participate in enriching activities outside of their classroom, such as **mentoring** another employee or organizing professional in-service sessions for other employees.

■ Creating work committees that consist of employees and administration. This gives employees the opportunity to participate in program projects, address center issues, and feel that they have a voice and that their opinions and ideas matter. Some examples of committees are morale committee, welcome wagon committee, employee wellness committee, employee satisfaction committee (which determines issues resulting from surveys and develops action plans), and health and safety committee.

Job Enrichment.   Job enrichment increases an employee's responsibility and control of his or her work demands. The goal is to increase efficiency and an employee's satisfaction by providing additional possibilities for personal achievement, recognition, challenge, responsibility, and individual growth and advancement in a job.

Many job enrichment programs rely on Frederick Herzberg's (1966) two-factor theory (see Chapter 2). Herzberg found that when employees described the times they felt good about their jobs, they tended to identify factors directly associated with the content of the job: achievement, recognition, the work itself, responsibility, and advancement. He concluded that the only way to make meaningful changes in work design was to include more of the following motivation factors:

■ *Accountability—Employees are held accountable for their own work performance.* Make sure that employee expectations are clear, performance feedback is given regularly, and all employees are consistently held accountable, including administration (Figure 5-5).

■ *Achievement—Employees feel that they are accomplishing something worthwhile.* Help employees understand the "big picture," including the program's goals and successes, and give them credit when they do so.

■ *Control over resources—Employees have control over their resources and costs; cost and profit centers are delegated to lower levels of the organization.* Implement a monthly classroom

Figure 5-5 Constructive feedback helps employees be accountable for their performance.

budget, so that each teacher has control over her or his own planning and supply purchases.

- *Feedback—Employees receive direct and timely information from the job itself about performance.* Help employees see the results of their work through the children's progress and learning, parent feedback, regulatory inspections or accreditation, and the achievement of classroom and program goals.

- *Personal growth and development—Employees have the opportunity to learn new skills.* Provide opportunities for growth through mentoring, special projects, participation on committees, and professional development opportunities.

- *Work pace—Employees are able to set their own work pace and have the flexibility to schedule breaks.* Look for opportunities to provide flexibility, such as offering a workweek of four 10-hour days or variable break schedules. A readily available float, or substitute staffing plan can allow employees to have time off when needed for work/life balance.

- *Client relationships—Employees develop a relationship with clients and know whether they are satisfied.* Building relationships with parents is critical to the success of any program. Invite parents to become involved through classroom participation, social events, parent advisory committees, parent conferences, open house, and other programs.

Job Exchange. Job exchange allows people to move from one job to another, which provides experience and helps employees develop a greater appreciation for different roles. It also creates flexibility and reduces boredom by engaging employees in a variety of activities. **Cross-training** through job exchange results in employees' acquiring a broader range of knowledge and experience, and also can improve teamwork among employees. The concept of job exchange may be more difficult to implement in early childhood programs because of the importance of maintaining teacher consistency. However, there are ways to make job exchange manageable:

- Exchange roles for short periods of time. For example, have employees trade places for one or two hours during key times of the day, so they get a true "flavor" of the new role.

- Try a job exchange day each month, during which only one employee trades places with another employee from a different area. The following month, two other employees from different areas swap roles. This is an excellent opportunity for employees to gain perspective and "walk a mile in someone else's shoes."

- Share and discuss employees' reactions to exchange experiences at team meetings.

- Exchange visits with neighboring early childhood programs. This allows employees to network with other early childhood professionals and to observe other facilities, educational philosophies, and program policies.

The challenge for the motivational leader is to design employees' jobs and work experiences so they incorporate numerous motivators and ensure that employees will be satisfied and inspired to perform their best work. For leaders considering a job redesign, Robertson and Smith (1985) recommend a six-step procedure for analyzing existing jobs.

Step One: Review the literature and other external data (training manuals, old job descriptions, etc.).

Step Two: Ask immediate managers about the responsibilities and tasks required to do the job well.

Step Three: Ask similar questions of current employees performing the job.

Step Four: Observe an employee who does the job well.

Step Five: Try to do the job yourself, but be careful not to attempt jobs that are dangerous or should be performed only by employees who have considerable experience.

Step Six: Write a job description detailing all of your findings.

It is also important to consider additional factors such as program policies, licensing regulations, incentives, and feedback that affect an employee's efficiency and motivation.

The Director's Showcase

What motivational strategies have you found effective in boosting staff morale?

"Several techniques that I use to boost staff moral include providing a buddy to mentor new staff members, helping staff identify professional development goals for the next year, and encouraging staff to become more involved in center activities, such as providing parent tours and presenting at staff development meetings."

Gail Kulick, Director
Alexian Brothers Childcare Center
Elk Grove Village, IL

Peer Mentoring

Mentoring is an effective training technique that can also be a valuable motivator. Peer mentoring involves pairing experienced employees with new or less experienced employees, in order to provide training, guidance, advice, and support (Bowden, 2004; Fraser, 1998). This approach has a number of distinct advantages. Inexperienced employees benefit from the mentor's knowledge and skills, while experienced employees gain a sense of pride and self-esteem from sharing their expertise. It also provides an opportunity to reinforce the mentors' own skills as they share them with others. Thus, mentoring provides professional growth and leadership skills for an experienced employee, helps the new employee gain direct experience in the workplace, provides accessible role modeling, develops peer-to-peer relationships, and increases the confidence of both employees (Pavia, Nissen, Hawkins, Monroe, & Filimon-Demyen, 2003).

When planning a mentoring program, be sure to set clear goals for both the mentor and the mentee (Figure 5-6). Develop an

Figure 5-6   Clear goals should be established for both the mentor and the mentee.

orientation checklist for new employees to ensure that all training items are covered, and follow up with both employees to be sure that effective training and communication have taken place.

Peer mentoring can also occur in other ways, such as an employee making a presentation at a staff meeting, conducting a training "lunch and learn" session, or sharing what he or she has learned after attending a conference. Employees may also identify their strengths and choose to mentor others in their areas of expertise, such as teaching creative arts, developing thematic units, or cooking with children.

Connecting Points: A mentor is not an exclusive or formal designation. A mentor can be anyone who influences change in others through example. Think about someone who has been a mentor to you.

- Why do you consider this person to be your mentor?
- What leadership qualities did the person demonstrate?
- What did you learn from him or her?
- What behaviors did you develop or change as a result of your relationship with this person?
- How has this relationship affected you personally and professionally?

Employee Empowerment

Empowerment is letting others assume the responsibilities, risks, and rewards associated with making their own decisions. Empowerment of employees encourages them to the take initiative to solve problems, gives them the freedom to get things done, provides the opportunity for professional growth, and helps the overall program run more smoothly (Pacini, 2000). Empowerment also reduces negativity, which typically occurs when employees feel helpless in identifying a solution or having any influence on organizational change.

True empowerment comes from within the individual, not from the leader. Motivational leaders create an environment that encourages employees to feel empowered to make decisions and take action. Ten actions for empowering employees have been suggested (Tracy, 1992).

- Tell people what their responsibilities are.
- Give them authority equal to their responsibilities.
- Set standards of excellence.
- Provide them with training.
- Give them knowledge and information.
- Provide them with feedback on their performance.
- Recognize them for their achievements.
- Trust them.
- Give them permission to fail.
- Treat them with dignity and respect.

Professional Development

The motivational leader understands that providing opportunities for paid professional development shows that you value and care enough about your employees to make an investment in their professional growth, while also investing in the quality of your program. Professional development energizes and motivates employees and enables them to network with other early childhood professionals. Even if the training program presents ideas or concepts that the employee has already learned or implemented, it can reinforce knowledge and skills. Examples of professional development opportunities that motivational leaders can support include:

- paid registration for local and state early childhood conferences or workshops.

- partial or full tuition reimbursement for college coursework or CDA training.

- membership to NAEYC and local early childhood resource and referral organizations.

- subscriptions to early childhood education journals.

- "lunch and learn" on-site training.

- on-site professional development days when the center is closed for employee training, team building, and classroom organization and preparation.

Reward System Evaluation

Motivational leaders understand that simply developing and implementing a reward system are not the final steps. Rewards, recognition, and encouragement must always be evaluated to determine their effectiveness in motivating employee behavior and achieving desired outcomes (Figure 5-7). What motivates an employee one

Figure 5-7 Motivators should always be evaluated for their effectiveness.

day may not prove to be motivating a week later, so leaders must continually assess employee needs, values, and personal goals. Conducting employee surveys or face-to-face meetings provides the motivational leader with valuable feedback regarding the effectiveness of ongoing initiatives.

Summary

- Reward systems that are meaningful and valued by the employee have a positive impact on behavior.
- Successful reward systems match the reward to the person, match the reward to the achievement, and are timely and specific.
- Intrinsic rewards are factors that cause employees to feel motivated by the work itself.
- Verbal recognition is the most valued form of praise and feedback for employees.
- Effective praise and feedback are timely, sincere, specific, and personal.
- Motivational leadership includes the provision of informal and formal feedback throughout the year.
- Job design offers many intrinsic rewards.
- Peer mentoring, employee empowerment, and professional development are effective reward systems that provide opportunities to expand the employee's role and provide professional growth.

Application Activities

1. List 10 situations in your workplace in which you have observed someone doing something special, such as helping two children settle a dispute or assisting a parent in locating a child's missing jacket. Write a positive feedback statement for the individual in each case, and record your responses on Application Worksheet 5-1.

2. Use the strategy of job design to rewrite your current job description. Repeat the exercise using job expansion and job enrichment. Use Application Worksheet 5-2 to develop and record your descriptions. When you are finished, select one of the options, and discuss why you prefer this choice.

3. Add your suggestions to those listed in the section "Simple Ways to Praise," and record them on Application Worksheet 5-3. Try out several of your suggestions on your colleagues and reflect on their responses.

4. Role-play with a partner the appropriate ways to give praise in each situation.

   a. A teacher offers to stay late so a fellow teacher can go to an appointment.

   b. The cook prepares a special meal for a child who is allergic to wheat.

   c. A teacher brings in his collection of seashells for a science project.

   d. A parent organizes a successful fund-raising event for the school.

Record your dialogue on Application Worksheet 5-4, and reflect on how effective the praise was in each situation.

Discussion Points

1. Discuss the likely consequences of having a leader who never provides any positive feedback.

2. Describe the concept of mentoring. What are the benefits?

3. Why are intrinsic rewards likely to have a more lasting effect on employee motivation than extrinsic rewards?

4. What are some things leaders can do to empower their employees? Why is empowerment important in the workplace?

5. Why must leaders evaluate their reward systems?

Application Worksheet 5-1

List 10 situations in your workplace in which you have observed someone doing something special. Write a positive feedback statement for the person in each situation.

1.

2.

3.

4.

5.

6.

7.

8.

9.

10.

Application Worksheet 5-2

Rewrite your current job description using *job design*.

Repeat this exercise using *job expansion*.

Repeat this exercise using *job enrichment*.

Select one of the options, and discus why you prefer this choice.

Application Worksheet 5-3

My suggestions for "Simple Ways to Praise"

Try several of your suggestions on your colleagues. How did they respond? Was it what you expected?

Application Worksheet 5-4

Record your positive praise responses in each situation.

a.

b.

c.

d.

Were you comfortable and confident using this strategy? Explain.

How successful were your statements in each situation? Have your colleagues critique your responses. Rewrite those that you feel need improvement.

References

Bowden, S. H. (2004). Top ten list for choosing to become a mentor. *Young Children, 59* (4), 78–79.

Fraser, J. (1998). *Teacher to teacher: A guide for effective mentoring.* Portsmouth, NH: Heinemann.

Herzberg, F. (1966). *Work and the nature of man.* Cleveland: World Publishing Co.

Lieberman, A. (1995). Practices that support teacher development. *Phi Delta Kappan, 76* (8), 591–96.

Luce, J. A. (1998, Fall). Career ladders: Modifying teachers' work to sustain motivation. *Education, 119* (1), 15–19.

Pacini, L. A. (2000). The power of empowerment. *Young Children, 55* (6), 83–85.

Pavia, L., Nissen, H., Hawkins, C., Monroe, M. E., & Filimon-Demyen, D. (2003). Mentoring early childhood professionals. *Journal of Research in Early Childhood Education, 17* (2), 250–260.

Robertson, I., & Smith, M. (1985). *Motivation and job design: Theory, research, and practice.* St. Paul, MN: West Publishing Co.

Tracy, D. (1992). *10 Steps to empowerment: A common-sense guide to managing people.* New York: Quill/William Morrow.

Web Resources

Business Owner's Toolkit	*www.toolkit.cch.com*
Management Library	*www.managementhelp.org*
Harvard Business School Publishing	*www.hbslink.org*

Chapter 6

Leadership Challenges: Looking Ahead

Objectives

After reading this chapter, you will be able to:

■ identify three trends that will challenge future early education leaders to practice a motivational style of leadership.

■ explain how generational differences affect the satisfaction of employees' motivational needs.

■ discuss how early childhood education and the business community can benefit from partnering.

■ explain why it is essential that leaders recruit teachers from diverse backgrounds.

Key Terms

■ Baby Boomers

■ constructive

■ Gen Xers

■ Generation Y

■ homogeneous

> *"A leader has the vision and conviction that a dream can be achieved. He inspires the power and energy to get it done."*
>
> RALPH LAUREN

Introduction

New and ongoing challenges will make it exceedingly important for leaders to practice a motivational style of leadership. For example, older employees are expected to remain in the workforce longer than in the past (Toossi, 2004). Some will stay in their present jobs, while others will look for part-time positions that provide a supplemental income as well as flexible schedules. Younger employees will enter the workforce with expectations that differ significantly from those of earlier generations. They will expect leaders to meet their motivational needs, or they will quickly move on (Chester, 2002). Consequently, leaders will need to dedicate quality time to learning more about their employees and listening carefully to their concerns. It will be necessary for them to establish and maintain an atmosphere of open communication in order to create workplace environments that foster productivity, commitment, and professional growth. In addition, successful leaders will find that investing time in acknowledging employees' contributions conveys a sense of caring that can translate into improved job satisfaction and employee retention.

In this final chapter, we will identify several emerging developments that successful early childhood leaders should understand and be prepared to address. Doing so will enable them to respond with motivational strategies that are both innovative and effective.

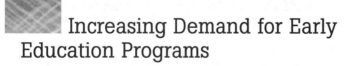 Increasing Demand for Early Education Programs

Recent predictions suggest that the demand for early education programs will continue to increase (Figure 6-1) (U.S. Department of Labor, 2005). More parents with young children, especially those with infants and toddlers, are expected to enter the workforce. Changes in welfare laws are also forcing many single mothers to seek gainful employment for the first time (Administration for Children and Families, 2000). A high percentage of these families will turn to community-based programs to provide care for their children while they are at work. Existing shortages, especially for infant and toddler care, combined with increased demand are likely to cause the early childhood market to undergo significant expansion.

Figure 6-1   Demand for early education programs continues to increase.

There are additional trends to consider. For example, parents are becoming more aware of the positive developmental outcomes associated with early learning opportunities. Favorable publicity is resulting in increased demands and support for more early education programs. States are beginning to earmark new funding so that school districts can add prekindergarten programs for three- and four-year-olds (Committee on Ways & Means, 2004). Nonprofit and for-profit early childhood programs are expanding their operations to serve more children. Additional programs are opening in a variety of nontraditional settings, including hospitals, gyms, sports clubs, casinos, shopping malls, and large corporate offices. Heightened concerns about children's safety are also causing more parents to enroll their older children in before- and after-school programs instead of leaving them alone at home.

All current indicators suggest that early childhood programs will experience continued growth and expansion (U.S. Department of Labor, 2005). This trend, combined with retirements and teachers who may decide to leave the field, will create additional employment opportunities for trained teachers.

The Director's Showcase

What motivational challenges are you currently facing in your program?

"I always wish I could pay my teachers more, and find additional time."

Candy Seltman, Administrative Director
Shawnee Mission Medical Center Child Care Center
Shawnee Mission, KS.

Business Partnerships and Economic Contributions

One of the most overlooked aspects of early childhood education has been the economic contribution these programs make to the local, state, and national economies (National Economic Development and Law Center, 2004; Texas Workforce Commission, 2003). A study conducted by the Center for the Child Care Workforce (2002) estimates that the annual number of paid child care providers (e.g., teachers, home-based providers, nonrelatives, and relatives) in the United States is approximately 2.5 million. Employee wages, school district savings derived from having children enrolled in early learning programs, improved graduation rates, and reduced crime rates have resulted in significant savings for local and state governments. Until recently, many of these successes have gone largely unrecognized. However, some policy makers are beginning to understand that financial investments made in early education programs can yield profits, and now they are using the evidence to promote changes in funding patterns.

The business community also stands to benefit when it invests in quality early childhood programs (Cubed, 2002). Many companies have discovered that offering employees access to early childhood education programs can be an effective recruiting and retention tool. In addition, they have noted that productivity typically increases, absenteeism rates improve, and employees are less distracted by concerns about their children's welfare (Baughman, DiNardi, & Holtz-Eakin, 2003). Ultimately, businesses will understand that when they partner with early childhood programs, they are investing in the education of children who will eventually become tomorrow's workforce.

Staffing

Motivational leaders will continue to face the challenging task of recruiting and retaining qualified teachers (Figure 6-2). However, the competition for talented staff is likely to intensify as the number of early childhood programs increases. With fewer students entering teacher training programs, older staff retiring, and other teachers making career changes, leaders will need to develop a repertoire of creative motivational strategies.

Changes are obviously needed if we are to meet increasing demands for teachers, new programs, and the delivery of quality services. Salary improvements and benefit packages, for example, are essential for attracting new teachers and enticing current staff to remain in their positions. Hiring part-time teachers, who may be in between jobs, attending school, or simply interested in working fewer hours or a more flexible schedule, offers another solution for addressing teacher shortages. Although this practice is becoming increasingly common in other work sectors, it has been shown to have some negative consequences for young children (NICHD, 1999). When programs hire part-time teachers to meet their staffing needs, motivational leaders must be willing to invest additional

Figure 6-2 Leaders are continually challenged to recruit and retain quality teachers.

time and effort in getting to know individual personnel so they feel valued and remain dedicated to the program.

Working with teachers from different generations will also present motivational leaders with challenges. Workplace environments and leadership practices may have to be modified to satisfy teachers who have grown up in different eras and have different motivational needs (Zemke, Raines, & Filipczak, 2000). For example, the **Baby Boomers,** born between 1946 and 1965, are currently nearing retirement, although many plan to remain in their jobs. Some Boomers will continue to work because they have children in college, are caring for aging parents, or have limited savings. Consequently, they are more likely to be motivated by the following:

- salary increases
- benefits, such as health and disability insurance
- special recognition, such as titles, designated parking space, awards, and ceremonies
- responsibility that acknowledges their experience, such as chairing a committee, mentoring new employees, or assuming leadership positions

Adults born between 1965 and 1980 have been labeled Generation Xers and are often characterized as informal, independent, questioning, adventuresome, and well educated (Raines, 2003). Unlike their predecessors, **Gen Xers** were raised in an era when it was often necessary for them to function independently because their parents were working, computers gave them immediate access to limitless information, and MTV provided fast-paced entertainment. As a result, Gen Xers are less likely to be motivated by monetary incentives and prefer the following instead:

- job flexibility, such as time off for personal appointments (e.g., dentist and doctor visits) or family events (e.g., children's performances, school conferences, funerals, and weddings) and part-time work
- job responsibilities that are challenging and meaningful, encourage independent work, and involve participation in decision making
- feedback that is immediate, specific, and **constructive;** immediate praise, spontaneous acknowledgements of their efforts, and incentives

- opportunities for career growth, including new job assignments, added responsibilities, and acquisition of new skills by attending trainings, classes, and conferences

- work environments and jobs that include fun, such as pizza parties, ice cream retreats, refreshments at meetings, celebration of special events such as birthdays and recent achievements, staff appreciation parties, and staff movie nights (renting a movie and serving refreshments)

Gen Xers are willing to work hard at things they find meaningful, but they want to have fun doing so (Figure 6-3).

The newest generation of workers, born between 1981 and 2000, has been labeled **Generation Y,** or the "Millennial Generation" (Chester, 2002). These employees often have considerable work experience because they have held part-time positions while completing school. In contrast to Gen Xers who value their independence, Generation Ys are more inclined to engage in mentoring relationships, where they can continue to learn from and socialize with other staff members. As a result, they are motivated

Figure 6-3 Gen Xers want meaningful work and to have fun doing it.

by the following:

- jobs that are meaningful and offer challenge without excessive stress
- opportunities to learn, such as participating in training sessions where they can develop new skills, partnering with a mentor, and enrolling in classes
- schedules that allow some flexibility and personal time off
- leaders who are sincere and treat them respectfully, giving credit for things they've accomplished and acknowledging their contributions in public places (e.g., newsletters, plaques, announcements, designated parking spaces)
- work environments that encourage and support innovation
- feedback that is frequent and constructive
- social occasions where they can interact with colleagues
- opportunities to mentor other staff members and to work together on teams

Thus, generational diversity will require leaders who are dedicated to treating employees as individuals and not as part of a **homogeneous** group.

Connecting Points: Think about your current employment situation.

- If your boss were to offer you a three-cent hourly raise, would you find this motivating? Explain why or why not.
- How would you feel if your boss offered your 50-year-old coworker a five-cent hourly raise but offered you one afternoon a month off instead? Which option would you prefer? Explain why.
- If you were your boss, what types of motivators would you find most rewarding?

 ## Population Diversity

The U.S. population consists of increasing ethnic and racial diversity as a result of immigration trends and continued growth among minority groups (U.S. Department of Labor, 1999). However, the majority of early education teachers do not reflect this trend (Rolfe, 2005). Although more children from diverse backgrounds are

Figure 6-4   Recruiting and retaining teachers of diverse backgrounds must be priorities.

attending early childhood programs, more than 75 percent of teachers are female Caucasians who are middle class and speak English only (Saluja, Early, & Clifford, 2002).

Efforts to recruit and retain qualified early childhood teachers and leaders from diverse backgrounds must become a priority (Figure 6-4) (Washington, 2005). Teachers who understand language barriers and cultural influences on children's development are able to create effective curricula and deliver them in ways that are meaningful for children. They also serve as important role models and help to dispel unacceptable stereotyping.

Unfortunately, the number of minority teachers is expected to decrease. Increasing tuition costs and financial aid reductions present barriers for many students of minority background who want to pursue an advanced degree (National Center for Education Statistics, 1998). Colleges and universities may be able to attract more students from diverse backgrounds to early childhood teacher training programs by increasing scholarship and campus support programs. Educators can also help students identify scholarship programs designated specifically for increasing teacher diversity. They should make students aware of loan-forgiveness programs currently available in many states.

Orientation training offers an important opportunity for new teachers, especially those from diverse backgrounds, to become familiar with program policies, procedures, and colleagues. Mentoring relationships with experienced teachers can help ease the newly hired teachers' transition and ensure early success (Schlank, 2004). Leaders should also devote time to identifying motivators that are culturally and racially sensitive, and meet teachers' individual needs for personal and professional growth. Understanding differences in dietary preferences, communication styles, and interests, for example, is essential if motivators are to be effective in retaining a diverse teaching staff.

The Director's Showcase

What do you think healthy employee morale should look like in your program?

"I consider employee morale healthy when they are engaged with children and their families and colleagues, and see themselves as integral to building the program's success. For example, one day a staff member noticed two elderly gentlemen who entered our child care facility and were apparently lost. She asked if they needed help locating the entrance to the physician's office, walked them to their destination, and then contacted the physician's receptionist to let her know where the gentlemen had parked their car so they could locate it afterward. Morale is obviously high with this individual and is reflected in her behavior."

Diane Schultz, Director
Family Services
BryanLGH Medical Center
Lincoln, NE

 ## Professional Development

We live in a world that is changing at an extremely rapid pace. New developments and technology appear on a daily basis. The challenge for early childhood leadership is to determine how to:

- help teachers remain current.
- foster improvements in teacher knowledge and experience.

- encourage receptiveness to new ideas.
- facilitate change.
- help teachers integrate new classroom practices to improve children's learning.

Educational preparation plays a major and direct role in addressing many of these issues (Hyson, 2001). Recall Maslow's highest level of needs, self-actualization, which was discussed in Chapter 2. Maslow believed that individuals have a need for self-fulfillment that is satisfied through the realization of their potentials. Motivational leaders can create supportive environments in which individuals have opportunities to attend classes and professional conferences, access relevant reading material, and assume new roles and responsibilities. These experiences can lead to acquisition of new skills, improved knowledge, and increased effectiveness, as well as a personal sense of accomplishment and self-actualization. Children, in turn, also benefit from having teachers who continue to grow professionally.

Many states have developed models of early childhood professional development, or career ladders, based on various levels of educational attainment. Establishing teacher qualifications is a critical step in the right direction. Not only will it lead to improvements in the quality of children's educational experiences, but it will also lend credibility to initiatives aimed at improving teacher salaries and professional recognition (Ackerman, 2005; NAEYC, 1998). Efforts to establish standards that are more consistent will also help to define the early education field for policy makers and public advocates.

Additionally, leaders must understand and embrace the concept of lifelong learning (Cross, 1992). Doing so enhances their ability to assist teachers in achieving educational goals by implementing supportive policies and practices, such as granting release time, arranging flexible work schedules, providing stipends, participating in tuition assistance programs, and linking salary increases to education and experience.

Motivational leaders must make professional development an ongoing priority in their programs. Furthermore, they must understand that one size doesn't fit all and that a teacher's needs are different at each stage of her or his career (Vartuli & Fyfe, 1993). Meaningful learning experiences build on existing skills and advance a teacher's expertise. For example, a novice teacher may be interested in developing new behavior management skills,

Figure 6-5 More professional development opportunities are becoming available online.

whereas a teacher with 15 years of classroom experience may be interested in learning how to use computers to foster children's discovery. As more options and new modes of delivery, including online training, become available, leaders will be able to tailor professional development opportunities to meet teachers' individual needs (Figure 6-5) (Robert, 2000).

In short, professional development is a necessary ingredient for recruiting and retaining highly qualified teachers and advancing the field of early education. To be effective, it must be developmentally appropriate, reflective of teachers' needs and interests, supportive of a program's educational goals and mission, and responsive to the needs of individuals to reach their personal and professional potentials.

 ## The Power of Motivation

Many positive changes are occurring in the field of early childhood education. Job opportunities continue to increase, public awareness and support for early education are gaining more and more

Figure 6-6 Improvements in teacher preparation and salaries are essential to improving program quality.

attention, initiatives to improve teacher preparation and salaries are in their early stages, and measures to enhance program quality are gradually catching on (Figure 6-6).

Many early childhood professionals would agree that this is only the beginning and that much remains to be done. Fiscal problems and competition from public and private entities will continue to pose challenges to existing programs. Strategies for improving teachers' educational preparation, salaries, benefits, and working conditions will necessitate new partnerships with the business community and local and state governments (Whitebrook & Eichberg, 2002). Families will expect programs to modify services to meet their changing needs. Efforts to attract and retain teachers from diverse backgrounds will require dedicated attention. Factors that motivate teachers to work in early education programs today may not be the same in years to come.

These issues must not be considered unsolvable problems, however. Rather, they offer rewarding opportunities for educating community leaders and policy makers. They provide unique occasions for advocating on behalf of children, families, and teachers, and a chance to participate in changes that are likely to reform the field as we know it today. Although progress may be slow at times and new initiatives may not pass initially, each experience ultimately contributes to a better solution. Throughout trials and tribulations, leaders who believe in and practice a motivational leadership style will serve as an inspiration to others. They will be effective in recruiting and retaining quality teachers and help to achieve greater recognition and stronger commitments for early education. They will be able to foster teachers' personal and professional growth and energize the early childhood educators who ultimately make a difference in young children's lives.

Summary

- Increased demand for early childhood programs will be driven by factors such as more parents in the workforce, greater recognition of the value of early education, benefits to the business community, and concerns for children's safety.
- Early education programs make significant contributions to local, state, and national economies; school districts save on intervention and remedial programs; and businesses experience improved retention and productivity rates.
- Efforts to recruit and retain qualified teachers are often hampered by poor salaries and challenging working conditions.
- Employees born during different eras are motivated by different things.
  - Baby Boomers prefer extrinsic rewards, such as salary increases, titles, and ceremonies.
  - Gen Xers prefer independence, flexibility, and opportunities for professional growth.
  - Generation Ys want meaningful work, feedback, and opportunities to develop new skills.
- Increasing numbers of teachers from diverse backgrounds must be hired to better meet children's needs.

- New trends will increase the need for professional development opportunities.
- Motivational leaders will continue to play a key role in boosting employee morale and ensuring program success.

Application Activities

1. Generate a list of professional development topics that could be used for in-service programs, and record your suggestions on Application Worksheet 6-1. Identify whether each topic is more appropriate for new (N) or experienced (E) teachers.

2. Develop a tool that could be used for evaluating the effectiveness of professional development training. Address issues such as audience learning, participant interest, appropriateness, and usefulness of the information. Use Application Worksheet 6-2 to outline your plan.

3. Use Application Worksheet 6-3 to draft a media release advocating community support for increased early education teacher salaries. What points are important for you to include?

Discussion Points

1. Discuss ways that your program might change to serve more children.

2. What are Gen Xers and Generation Ys? What motivational needs do you expect them to share? How do their motivational needs differ?

3. Why is it important that early education programs recruit and hire teachers from diverse backgrounds?

4. What do you see as future challenges to early education programs and leadership?

Application Worksheet 6-1

Prepare a list of topics that are useful and appropriate for professional development training. Identify whether each topic is more appropriate for new or novice teachers (N) or for those who are experienced (E).

What would you do if your staff believed they already knew enough about a topic but you felt they could benefit from additional information? How would you resolve this situation? What would you do to assure them that they would learn something from attending?

Application Worksheet 6-2

What evaluation criteria does your professional development evaluation tool include?

How should evaluation feedback be used to improve the quality of future training?

Professional development evaluation forms often include statements about the room (e.g., temperature, noise, comfort), food, and location. Do you think these are important items to assess? Explain.

Application Worksheet 6-3

What key points are important to address in the media release?

How would the media release read?

How can you determine whether your statement was effective?

How would different types of media (e.g., television, radio, fliers, mar-quee, bulletin board) influence the nature of your media release? Choose two different media forms, and rework your statement so that it is appro-priate for each.

References

Ackerman, D. (2005). Getting teachers from here to there: Examining issues related to an early care and education teacher policy. *Early Childhood Research & Practice, 7* (1). Retrieved on December 10, 2005, from http://ecrp.uiuc.edu.

Administration for Children and Families. (2000). *The national study of child care for low-income families.* U.S. Department of Health and Human Services, Administration for Children and Families. Retrieved on December, 10, 2005, from http://www.acf.dhhs.gov/programs/ccb/research/ccprc/lowincom/index.htm.

Baughman, R., DiNardi, D., & Holtz-Eakin, D. (2003). Productivity and wage effects of "family-friendly" fringe benefits. *International Journal of Manpower, 24* (3), 247–259.

Center for the Child Care Workforce. (2002). *Estimating the size and components of the U. S. child care workforce and caregiving population: Key findings from the child care workforce estimate.* Washington, DC: Author.

Chester, E. (2002). *Employing generation why?* Golden, CO: Chess Press.

Committee on Ways & Means. (2004). *Green Book; Section 9, Child Care.* Washington, DC: U.S. House of Representatives. Retrieved on August 20, 2005, from http://waysandmeans.house.gov/Documents.asp?section=813.

Cross, P. (1992). *Adults as learners: Increasing participation and facilitating learning.* San Francisco: Jossey-Bass.

Cubed, M. (2002). *The national economic impacts of the child care sector.* Washington, DC: National Child Care Association. Retrieved on August, 8, 2005, from www.nccanet.org/NCCA%20Impact%20Study.pdf.

Hyson, M. (2001). Better futures for young children, better preparation for their teachers: Challenges emerging from recent national reports. *Young Children, 56* (1), 60–62.

National Association for the Education of Young Children. (1998). *A conceptual framework for early childhood professional development.* Retrieved on September 3, 2005, from http://www.naeyc.org/about/positions/PSCONF98.asp.

National Center for Education Statistics. (1998). *Digest of educational statistics.* Washington, DC: Author.

National Economic Development and Law Center (NEDLC). (2004). *The economic impact of the child care and early education industry in Massachusetts.* Oakland, CA: Author.

NICHD Early Child Care Research Network. (1999). Child outcomes when child care center classes meet recommended standards for quality. *American Journal of Public Health, 89,* 1072–1977.

Raines, C. (2003). *Connecting generations: The sourcebook for a new workplace.* Mississauga, Ontario: Crisp Learning.

Robert, C. (2000). Distant places, diverse spaces: Early childhood professional development in isolated locations. *Contemporary Issues in Early Childhood, 1* (3), 277–286.

Rolfe, H. (2005). Building a stable workforce: Recruitment and retention in the child care and early years sector. *Children & Society, 19* (1), 54–65.

Saluja, G., Early, D., & Clifford, R. (2002). Demographic characteristics of early childhood teachers and structural elements of early care and education in the United States. *Early Childhood Research & Practice, 4* (1), 1–18.

Schlank, C. (2004). Teachers on teaching: To teach until we die. *Young Children, 59* (2), 67–70.

Texas Workforce Commission. (2003). *The economic impact of the child care industry in Texas.* Austin, TX: Author. Retrieved on August 28, 2005, from http://www.texasworkforce.org.

Toossi, M. (2004, February). Labor force projections to 2012: The graying of the U.S. workforce, *Monthly Labor Review, 127* (2), 37–57.

U.S. Department of Labor. (1999). *Futurework - Trends and challenges for work in the 21st century.* Washington, DC: Author. Retrieved on August 28, 2005, from http://www.dol.gov/asp/programs/history/herman/reports/futurework/execsum.htm.

U.S. Department of Labor. (2005). *Occupational outlook handbook, 2004–05 edition, childcare workers.* Washington, DC: U.S. Department of Labor, Bureau of Labor Statistics. Retrieved on September 20, 2005, from http://www.bls.gov/oco/cg/cgs032.htm.

Vartuli, S., & Fyfe, B. (1993). Teachers need developmentally appropriate practices too. *Young Children, 48* (4), 36–42.

Washington, V. (2005). Sharing leadership: A case study of diversity in our profession. *Young Children, 60* (1), 23–31.

Whitebrook, M., & Eichberg, A. (2002). Finding the better way: Defining and assessing public policies to improve the child care workforce. *Young Children, 57* (3), 66–72.

Zemke, R., Raines, C., & Filipczak, B. (2000). *Generations at work: Managing the clash of veterans, boomers, Xers, and nexters in your workplace.* New York: American Management Association Publications.

Web Resources

BusinessTown	*www.businesstown.com/*
The Future of Children	*www.futureofchildren.org*
National Child Care Information Center	*www.nccic.org*
NAEYC Accreditation Project	*www.naeyc.org*

Appendices

Appendix A

Survival Kits

 Teacher Survival Kit

Print the following statements on cute themed stationery and attach them to large, clear bags filled with the items in the list. On each bag, write "This bag of goodies is to help remind you of the many ways that you make a difference in the lives of the children, and how important you are to our team!"

HERSHEY HUG—to bring you some encouragement.

SMILE STICKER—to remind you that a positive attitude makes a difference!

PACKET OF FLOWER SEEDS—to represent teaching. You plant the seeds for learning and social development every day. The children, just like these seeds, need tender loving care to grow and blossom.

RUBBER BAND—to remind you of how far you can stretch and the need to be flexible with others.

QUARTER—to remind you that it's okay to call for help.

SNICKERS—to help you keep your sense of humor.

PENNY—for your thoughts. They are important!

BALLOON—for when you feel like blowing off some hot air.

TOOTHPICK—to remind you to pick out the good in others and yourself.

SUGAR PACKET—to remind you to be sweet.

ERASER—for when you make mistakes. Remember, we all make mistakes, and the important thing is that we learn from them.

STARBURST—for when you need an extra burst of energy.

HIGHLIGHTER—to remind you to focus on the joys and highlights of each day.

RECIPE CARD—to write down the main ingredients for successful teamwork—your thoughts and ideas—and then share them with us.

PUZZLE PIECE—without you, our team is not complete!

 ## Team Builders Survival Kit

Print the following statements and attach them to clear bags filled with items from the list.

BIT O' HONEY—to remind you to keep from saying hurtful things to others. Share a bit o' honey!

LIFESAVER—to remind you that your actions can be a lifesaver to a child, parent, or fellow team member.

TOOTHPICK—to remind you to pick out the best in others.

100 GRAND CANDY BAR—to remind you that you are worth more than 100 grand to us!

ERASER—to remind you that we all make mistakes and need to erase our errors with an apology.

CRAYON—to remind you that it takes all colors to make a rainbow. The unique skills and talents of each individual make a stronger team.

MOUNDS CANDY BAR—for the mounds of wisdom you have to pass on to others.

GUM—for when you feel like chewing on someone, but know this would be best.

RUBBER BAND—to remind you that we all need to band together as a team for success.

PLASTIC BAG—a good role model will hold these ideas together, just as this bag holds these items together.

Become a team player and make a difference!

Wellness Survival Kit

Print the poem and attach it to a mug filled with the items suggested.

It's that time of year again,
Those sickly little bugs!
Taking care of self is key
To keep giving all those little hugs!

Little noses needing wiped,
Sniffles, coughs, and flu.
Wash your hands to prevent those germs,
You're bound to catch a few!

Vitamin C, hot tea,
Relax and get some rest!
Have some soup, read a book.
We hope you'll feel your best!

Suggested Items to Include in the Mug

- Herbal tea bags
- Vitamin C drops
- Cough drops
- Kleenex
- Package of dry soup mix
- Hot chocolate or apple cider mix
- Hand sanitizing gel

 # Stress Busters Survival Kit

Print the words of advice on a card and attach it to a cheery gift bag filled with the items suggested.

Feeling stressed? The best cure for stress is laughter, play, and moments of relaxation. Adults need to remember to take "time out" from stress and create moments of enjoyment. Make it a great day!

Suggested Items to Include in the Gift Bag

- Chocolate
- Bubbles (to blow)
- Play dough
- Stress ball
- Water motion toy
- Word game/puzzle book
- Humor book relating to working with children
- Lotion
- Bath bubbles
- Scented candle
- CD of relaxing music

Note: You can find inexpensive CDs at used book/music stores, bulk toys through party supply companies, and bath products at discount stores. Watch clearance sales for other relaxing items.

 ## New Teacher Survival Kit

A new teacher survival kit can be a combination of the preceding kits with the following suggested items. To make this kit more festive, place the items in a basket, which can be very inexpensive if purchased at craft stores and sales, and decorate the basket with ribbon.

- Staff handbook
- Parent handbook
- Orientation checklist
- Training schedule
- Organization chart
- List of staff with assigned classrooms/work areas and work schedules
- Center mission statement, philosophy, and goals
- Handouts regarding child development topics such as developmentally appropriate practice, positive guidance, and positive ways to talk with children and parents
- Hand lotion
- Leftover fund-raiser item such as a child care center T-shirt or cookbook

Appendix B

Motivation Assessment Tools

Strengths and Work Preference Survey

My work style preferences are (check all that apply):

☐ I prefer frequent, hands-on guidance/direction from my supervisor.

☐ I prefer to work independently or one on one with feedback regarding end results.

☐ I prefer to work in a team with participation and feedback from others throughout the process.

☐ I prefer to work with ideas and data.

☐ I prefer to work mostly with people.

☐ I prefer a structured work environment.

☐ I prefer a changing, flexible work environment with variety.

☐ I prefer to take risks.

☐ I prefer to play it safe.

☐ I am open to change (positive or negative).

☐ Change is not easy for me.

☐ I am willing to take on additional responsibilities.

☐ I am willing to lead others and take charge of projects or committees.

Please list any special skills or talents that you are willing to contribute (examples: music, artistic abilities, hobbies, etc.): _____

_____

_____

I am interested in participating in the center in the following ways (check all that apply):

☐ Mentor a new employee.

☐ Teach a "lunch and learn" workshop. Topic: _____

☐ Participate on a center committee: _____

☐ Be a teacher representative on the Parent Advisory Committee.

☐ Organize an appreciation or team-building event.

☐ Other: _____

Employee Recognition Preference Survey

Each of us likes to be recognized in different ways. Please tell us how you would like to be recognized and what you are willing to do to help make our workplace a more supportive environment.

Rank the following in order of preference; leave items blank that are not of interest.

☐ Public praise (center newsletter, staff meeting, bulletin board, etc.)

☐ Verbal praise given in person

☐ Note of appreciation from manager

☐ Note of appreciation from peers

☐ Letter of recognition for personnel file, copy to supervisor

☐ A small personalized gift (example: coffee mug, certificate, lapel pin)

☐ Food items—suggestions: _____

☐ Opportunity to attend training of choice

☐ Opportunity to participate on committees and special projects

☐ Lunch with supervisor

☐ Nomination for unit awards for service excellence (examples: process improvement, customer service, safety, attendance, cost-saving ideas)

☐ Other (please describe) _____.

Check each box that applies.

☐ I am willing to participate in a peer-to-peer recognition program that helps me recognize my coworkers' efforts.

☐ I am willing to serve on a committee to develop and maintain recognition in our workplace.

Suggestions for other ways to show appreciation to all staff: _____

_____

_____

_____

Human Scavenger Hunt

Fill in each blank with the name of a coworker who fits the description. Each person may have only one description.

_____ has worked at the center for more than 10 years.

_____ has worked at the center for less than 1 year.

_____ drives more than 30 miles to work (one way).

_____ lives within 1 mile of the center.

_____ has more than three grandchildren.

_____ was born in another country.

_____ has lived in a coastal state.

_____ has been to the top of the Statue of Liberty.

_____ graduated from a Big 12 college.

_____ has been in the field of early childhood education for more than 25 years.

_____ participates in a recreational sports team.

_____ enjoys scrapbooking as a hobby.

_____ sings in a choir.

_____ has performed as a public speaker.

_____ has a child in college.

_____ has driven across the Golden Gate Bridge.

_____ was raised on a farm.

_____ plays a musical instrument.

_____ is a voracious reader.

 ## Getting to Know You

Please complete the following form, which will be kept in a note-book in the employee lounge and may be used as a reference for team-building activities or special events.

Name:

Birthday:

Anniversary:

Birthplace:

Family members:

Pets:

Favorite foods/snacks/desserts:

Hobbies:

Items I collect:

Years in early childhood education:

Education background:

Retirement dream:

What brings me joy:

I feel a sense of accomplishment when:

Birthday Buddy

Please fill out the attached form and return it to (insert name of Birthday Buddy Coordinator). Each person who chooses to participate will be assigned to a Birthday Buddy. On your buddy's birthday, please surprise him or her with a favorite drink, a favorite treat, or a little gift. You will receive the same in return on your birthday. This works only if everyone keeps up their end, so mark your calendars! Please return this form by (insert date).

Your name _____

Your birthday _____

Your favorite sweet _____

Your favorite drink _____

Your favorite hobby _____

Something you enjoy or like to collect _____

Suggestions _____

(*Note to reader:* You may want to set a price range for gifts.)

Secret Pal/Secret Santa

Please fill out the attached form and return it to (insert name of Secret Pal/Santa Coordinator). The more specific you are when filling out the information below, the more it will help your Secret Pal/Santa get something you will enjoy. When all the names have been collected, you will draw a name out of the hat and keep it a *secret* until the last day, when Secret Pals/Santas are revealed.

Each day (Monday through Thursday), you will give a small, thoughtful gift such as an encouraging note with a candy bar, soda, ornament, or small "trinket." These gifts will be given anonymously. Friday's gift will be a little larger. You will put your name on Friday's gift, so the person knows the identity of her or his Secret Pal/Santa!

Please use the information below and be thoughtful when choosing your gifts. Give things that you would enjoy and be happy to receive. If you don't feel like you know your person well enough, it's always a good idea to discreetly ask a coworker. Have fun!

Turn this form in by: (insert date)
Secret Pal/Santa Week: (insert dates)

_____

Your name _____

Your birthday _____

Your favorite sweet _____

Your favorite drink _____

Your favorite hobby _____

Something you enjoy or like to collect _____

_____

Suggestions _____

_____

(*Note to reader:* You may want to set a price range for gifts.)

Appendix C

Effective Feedback Dialogue Points

Providing feedback to employees is an essential element of leadership. The following dialogue points, or statements, can be used as a guide in feedback discussions.

Be direct and get to the point.

I asked you here to discuss . . .
I need to talk to you about . . .

State the purpose for the meeting.

I have a concern about . . .
A problem has occurred in . . .
It has been brought to my attention . . .
I want to share my recent classroom observations with you.

Describe what you know.

I saw . . .
When I was told . . ., I looked into the issue by . . .

Describe how you feel about what you know.

I am concerned about . . .
I am confused about why . . .
I was impressed to see . . .

Describe the impact of the problem.

If this continues, then . . .
If I were to look at this situation as a parent (customer), it would appear . . .

Encourage the other party to give his or her side of the story.

That is what I know about the situation. Please tell me your view.
Help me understand . . .
Is that the way you saw it?

Ask questions to understand the situation from the other person's perspective.

How do you know this information?
And then what happened?

Restate (in your own words) what the other person has said to you to ensure understanding.

If I understand correctly, you . . .
So, from your perspective, you . . .

Determine the next steps: what specific actions must be done, when, and by whom.

Tell me what steps you think would help to improve this situation.
What would you do differently next time?
I believe you will need to . . .
In the next week, we will . . .

Summarize the discussion.

Let's recap.
Our goal moving forward will be . . .
You have agreed to . . ., and I will . . .

Express your appreciation for the other person's efforts.

Thank you for listening to this concern with an open mind.
I appreciate your willingness to . . .
Your efforts to address this will be greatly appreciated.

Follow up.

I will contact you next.
Let's meet again on . . .

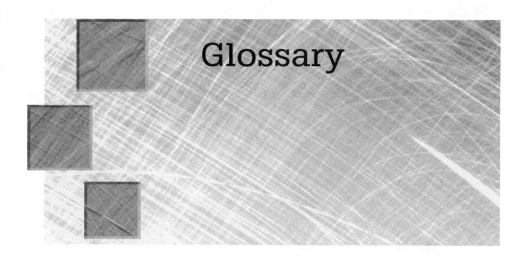

Glossary

A

accountable—responsible or liable for answering

attributes—personal qualities or characteristics

attrition—the loss of employees due to intentional choice, death, or retirement

autocratic—a form of leadership in which leaders maintain full control of all decisions and limit or restrict employees' input

B

Baby Boomers—persons born between 1946 and 1965

burnout—a physical or emotional response to prolonged stress; often results in a lack of interest and commitment

C

collaborative—to work together, especially in a joint intellectual effort

collegiality—a relationship based on respect and shared goals that is established among fellow employees

conflict resolution—the process of resolving a dispute or disagreement

constructive—helpful, includes suggestions for improvement

consultative—a leadership style in which leaders listen to employees' suggestions before making decisions

credibility—the quality, capability, or power to elicit belief

cross-training—instruction in different tasks or skills

D

definitive—final or conclusive

demographic—a statistical description of various human population characteristics, such as the number of employed fathers or the number of children per family

E

empowerment—invested with power or confidence; equipped or supplied with an ability; enabled

environment—the sum of an individual's surroundings

extrinsic motivators—tangible rewards that a person finds satisfying, such as a pay raise, designated parking space, a birthday gift, or movie tickets

F

feedback—an evaluative response; information about one's performance

G

Generation Y—persons born between 1981 and 2000

Gen Xers—persons born between 1965 and 1980

H

homogeneous—similar or alike

hygienes—a term used by Herzberg to describe working conditions

I

incentives—things that serve to induce or motivate

in-service—an activity that takes place or continues while one is a full-time employee

intrinsic motivators—rewards that provide an internal feeling of satisfaction, such as receiving a job promotion or praise, or being named employee of the month

invested—devoted morally or psychologically to a purpose; committed

L

laissez-faire—a form of leadership in which leaders provide employees with little or no guidance

M

mentoring—serving as a trusted counselor or teacher

mission—an inner calling to pursue an activity or perform a service

morale—an individual's or group's emotional state; degree of excitement or commitment

motivation—a perceived need that shapes the purpose and direction of a person's behavior

P

participative—a leadership style in which leaders encourage and respect employees' participation in decision-making activities

physiological needs—basic functions that must be satisfied for survival

productivity—the ability to understand a task, marshal resources, and complete the task in an efficient and timely manner

punitive—punishing or negative

R

regression—a retreat or moving backward

retention—keeping or retaining employees

retreat—a place affording peace, quiet, privacy, or security

S

self-actualization—the satisfaction an individual derives from using personal skills and talents

stress—a sense of frustration, tension, or anxiety that may develop when what a person expected to happen differs from what actually occurs

subjective—relating to a belief, bias, or interpretation that is not based on fact

T

T.E.A.C.H.—the Teacher Education and Compensation Helps program begun in 1990 and currently available in many states, through which early childhood teachers can apply for scholarships to advance their training and complete a degree

traits—characteristics unique to an individual

transactional—a leadership style characterized by the outcomes or accomplishments resulting from a leader's efforts; product orientation

transformational—a leadership style that reflects a leader's concern with the processes involved in achieving outcomes; process orientation

turnover rate—the number of employees who quit their positions in a given program or organization each year

V

values—worth in usefulness or importance to the possessor; utility or merit

W

WAGE$—a program designed to improve retention rates by offering additional salary compensation to teachers, home-based providers, and administrators based on their educational levels